MALTA
SPITFIRE
THE BUZZ BEURLING STORY
Canada's World War II Daredevil Pilot

FLYING OFFICER GEORGE F. BEURLING
DSO, DFC, DFM and Bar
with
LESLIE ROBERTS

Foreword by
AIR VICE-MARSHAL W. A. BISHOP
VC, DSO, MC, DFC, RCAF

Introduction by
WING-COMMANDER P. B. LUCAS
DSO. DFC

Illustrated by
CLAYTON KNIGHT

New Epilogue by
ARTHUR BISHOP
RCAF Pilot and author of *Unsung Courage 1939–1945*

Penguin Books

PENGUIN

Published by the Penguin Group

Penguin Books Canada Ltd, 10 Alcorn Avenue, Toronto, Ontario, Canada M4V 3B2
Penguin Books Ltd, 80 Strand, London WC2R 0RL, England
Penguin Putnam Inc., 375 Hudson Street, New York, New York 10014, U.S.A.
Penguin Books Australia Ltd, 250 Camberwell Road, Camberwell, Victoria 3124,
Australia
Penguin Books (NZ) Ltd, cnr Rosedale and Airborne Roads, Albany, Auckland 1310,
New Zealand

Penguin Books Ltd, Registered Offices: Harmondsworth, Middlesex, England

First published by Farrar and Rinehart Inc., New York, 1943
Published by The Military Book Society, London, 1973
Published in Penguin Books, by Penguin Books Canada Limited, 2002

1 3 5 7 9 10 8 6 4 2

Original Copyright © George F. Beurling and Leslie Roberts, 1943
Published by arrangement with Lionel Leventhal Ltd.
Epilogue Copyright © Arthur Bishop, 2002

Printed and bound in Canada

NATIONAL LIBRARY OF CANADA CATALOGUING IN PUBLICATION DATA

Beurling, George F. (George Frederick), 1921–1948
Malta spitfire, the Buzz Beurling story : Canada's World War II daredevil pilot

Previously published under title: Malta spitfire : the story of a fighter pilot.
ISBN 0-14-301237-1

1. Beurling, George F. (George Frederick), 1921–1948.
2. Fighter pilots—Canada—Biography.
3. World War, 1939–1945—Personal narratives, Canadian.
4. World War, 1939–1945—Aerial operations, British.
5. World War, 1939–1945—Campaigns—Malta.
I. Roberts, Leslie, 1896– II. Title.

D811.B47 2002   940.54'4941'92   C2002-900970-7

Visit Penguin Canada's website at **www.penguin.ca**

Contents

INTRODUCTION

High summer, 1942 . . . The noonday sun blazes down on the parched Island. Heatwaves shimmer across the dusty, crater-marked airfield of Takali. 249 Squadron, on readiness since dawn, is about to stand down. New Zealanders, a South African, a Rhodesian, an American, Englishmen, a Scot, Canadians—all marvellously united by weeks of unrelenting combat—look forward to the respite. It has been an active morning.

The Adjutant comes down to the dispersal hut with the names of half a dozen new pilots who have just landed from Gibraltar. 249 is to get two replacements.

One of my Flight Commanders runs his eye down to the list. 'George Beurling', he exclaims, 'well, well . . . flew with us back in England in the North Weald wing; sergeant pilot, Canadian, good eyes, quick, aggressive. Not much discipline in the air, tends to get separated from the Squadron. Very individualistic; but he's got flair'.

'Would he fit in in 249?' I ask. 'Might do', comes the studied reply, 'but it's a risk. He'll either shoot some down or "buy it".'

An hour or so later, a fair, tousled-headed young man with restive, ice-blue eyes and the look of a Scandinavian, is in my room reporting for squadron duty.

I take to him; extrovert, enthusiastic, lively. The customary exchanges end with a timely admonition. 'Listen,' I caution, 'here on the Island we fly line abreast in pairs and fours of aircraft; never in line astern. Two or four pairs of eyes looking inwards cover the whole sky. If you get separated find another aircraft and join up quickly. There are more Me 109's out here than Spitfires.'

'The goddam screwballs!'

Those three words were to become a legend in the days and weeks which followed.

P. B. Lucas
Spring 1973

Foreword

EVERY man who flew in the First World War will glow with pride as he reads the story of George Beurling's exploits in the second. To me, it has been like going back to the job of knocking the Hun out of the skies by proxy. Reading of his dogfights, his sweeps and scrambles, his many victories and occasional misfortunes has been to see it all again as we knew the war in the clouds in other days. At first these stories came through piecemeal through our newspapers, a bit here and there. Now the whole panorama is unfolded, as George Beurling himself saw it, through his own eyes. It is signally important that this story should be told, in Beurling's own words, while the impact of the Battle of Malta is still sharp in his mind, because it is probably the greatest air story to come out of any front in the war, or out of any war fought since the coming of air power.

Maybe we who flew the Nieuports, the Camels, Spads and Se5s of another day envy George and all the other lads who fly the Spitfires today. In the back of our minds we probably wonder how we would have done at the controls of the fighters of 1943. One thing is sure, every man of us thrills with pride as he looks at the record of the new generation of sky-fighters, the lads from the Battle of Britain, from Malta, from the Pacific, from the East, Near and Far. They have carried the torch the old-timers handed on—carried it higher than we ever dreamed it could be held.

No story to come out of the war can excel that of this young Canadian who literally had to fight his way into the service. Any ordinary youngster would have thrown in his hand at any one of half a dozen stages of the journey: when the United States immigration authorities turned him back when he was on his way to China, when parental permission to enlist with the Finns was refused, when the Royal Canadian Air Force turned him down, and finally, when the Royal Air Force in Britain pointed out that he couldn't be taken in without a birth certificate. But Beurling stuck it out, and finally his chance came. Then, in fourteen glorious fighting days, he compiled an incredible record of victories over the Hun that gives every Canadian a thrill. But those victories were not scored for Canada alone. They were chalked up for Britain, for the British Empire, for the United States, for Russia, for China, for all the United Nations and for Malta. They were scored for the cause of Freedom, everywhere in the world. Flying Officer Beurling is essentially an individualist. What he has done is for the freedom of the individual, no matter where he may be. More power to his guns!

As one of the old-timers, then, I salute Canada's young falcon of Malta. That salute, I trust, will be accepted as coming from all the fliers of my generation who fought the First World War, to all the gallant youngsters who are flying, fighting, and winning this war.

W. A. BISHOP

Introduction

THIS book is about a young man with a single-track mind who has compiled what promises to stand as the all-over aerial record of the war: twenty-seven German and Italian aircraft destroyed in combat, eight others damaged, and three more scored as Probably Destroyed in fourteen fighting days over Malta! It is the story of a youngster who *knew* that, given the opportunity, he could be a peerless fighter pilot. It is the story, as well, of the opposition, no less tremendous because it was offered unconsciously, which he had to break down before he could prove his point —and of how, once he had broken through, he won four decorations for courage in the face of the enemy, plus an officer's commission, within the space of two months.

Some of Beurling's examiners have spoken of him in print as a cold-blooded killer. That, to my way of thinking, is as fantastic as it would be to picture him as a cozy sentimentalist. Wondering about that, wondering if my own assessment had gone askew as a result of close association, I asked Clayton Knight's opinion. How did Clayton size him up? What did Clayton think of the picture of a ruthless young man, shooting Germans out of the skies with almost maniacal sang-froid? Knight summed it in these words:

"To me he is a lad who is nuts about flying and completely preoccupied with the precise technique of flying and severely critical of sloppy flying by anybody else, be he German, Italian *or* British. He is only a killer in that he has schooled himself to be technically perfect, which means that he holds off for the necessary fraction of a second before firing—the fraction of a second that makes the difference between perfection and the waste of ammunition, brought on by sloppiness or panic."

There isn't a word I can add to that. It explains much of what you will read in these pages.

A word as to this book. When I was asked to become George's collaborator in its preparation, I undertook the task believing (I have no doubt) that I was tackling what might be called "another war hero story." I soon discovered my mistake. I was dealing with a young man whose very single-minded simplicity made him highly complex. Flying has been an obsession with George Beurling since he shed his diapers. There has never been anything else. But if I were to give him to you as the completely impersonal young man with an obsession, I'd be wrong. Weeks of living and working with him leave me with the feeling that I have been putting in time with an extremely lovable guy. That the qualities which make him lovable are not those which endear other men to me makes him no whit less lovable.

As to this collaboration between a flier and a flier-turned-writer, you may take it as gospel that it has been a collaboration in every sense of the term. This is no writing job cooked up from hurried examination of logbooks, or from cursory conversations. It is the result of seventeen solid days of living together, during which Beurling and I covered the span of his years from the day when he heard the sound of his first airplane motor to his incarceration in hospital, after being shot down into the Mediterranean. ("My own damned fault," says George. "A plain case of Pilot Error. I should have been taken out and shot for it!") From that seventeen-day grind this book emerged in what may be called its basic form. The rest was primarily a retouching job. The lingo and idiom are Beurling's, his own strange mixture of North American and British flying terms. The narrative is his. That is for the record, from a writer who has no respect of any sort for ghosting. Well, nobody ghosted George Beurling. This is his own story, as *he* talks it.

Thanks go from this corner to Air Vice-Marshal L. D. D. McKeen, C.B., O.B.E., Liaison Officer-in-Chief of the United Kingdom Air Mission to Canada, to Henry Jones, Esq., C.M.G., M.C., Civil Liaison Officer of the United Kingdom Air Mission, and to my old friend Group Captain H. R. Stewart, Director of Intelligence, Royal Canadian Air Force, for invaluable assistance and advice with the manuscript, with particular reference to what should *not* be said, for fear of the comfort and aid it might bring to the enemy. That was their only yardstick. Thanks go, as well, to numerous officers of the Royal Canadian Air Force Public Relations Branch for the manner in which, as always, they have made a writing man's job easier to do.

LESLIE ROBERTS

Montreal, Canada
June, 1943

Part One

CHAPTER I

To the Stars the Hard Way

IT WASN'T an easy war to get into, back in 1939 and 1940. In fact, if you lived in Canada and wanted to fly, you soon began to think it must be a private war, reserved for university graduates, or people with brown hair, or former glass blowers, but certainly not open to young men whose principal qualification was a desire to get in there and fight. Later you found that the trouble had been a lack of planes and schools and instructors, that the country wasn't organized for the job it had taken on. But you didn't know that at first and you hadn't realized that you wouldn't be allowed to fight Germans in the air unless you could prove that you had gone all the way through high school. It fried you to a crisp to learn these things, not to be able to get in, to feel that you were being barred from the job you had been living for, that you were all raveled in red tape. That was the way it hit me— and plenty of others.

Ever since I can remember, airplanes and to get up in them into the free sky had been the beginning and end of my thoughts and ambitions. The woods are full of youngsters who drop anything they're doing to watch the planes go by and who can tell by the drone of an engine exactly what type of aircraft is passing. All over North America kids by the tens of thousands are whittling flying models. But with me it went even deeper than that. I don't know exactly when I began to feel this way, by the time I was nine all my afterschool hours and my Saturdays were spent at the old Lasalle Road Airport, about three miles from home, watching the planes of the Montreal Light Aeroplane Club and others—I remember seeing a couple of Gypsy Moths, an Aironca and a Travelair— I remember seeing them take off and land.

I realize that even then flying was an obsession with me. From the first day I watched a Moth disappear beyond the St. Lawrence I knew I was going to be a pilot, or else. Instead of sitting behind my desk in Bannantyne School, the urge to sneak off to the airport was too strong and I'd play hooky, knowing the cost only too well—two lickings, one at school and another at home—but I figured it was well worth it. When I got out to the field I'd climb the fence and try to get near the planes, hoping I'd maybe even get a chance to talk to a pilot. Then, in the late afternoon, I'd sneak home, late for supper, and afterwards put in hours of homework on the newest model aircraft hidden in the bedroom cupboard.

"COME ON IN, KID, AND KEEP DRY," HE SAID

That year the Lasalle Airport was closed down and the planes moved out behind Mount Royal, back of the city, to the Cartierville field. I was only nine or ten then, and it was a long trek, but I was out there every Saturday, and whenever else I could make it. Sometimes I was lucky enough to scrape up a couple of streetcar tickets. But no matter how I got there, I'd be at the field whenever I could, just hanging around, watching and hoping. Then, all of a sudden, the dream came true.

It was during the summer holidays, the year I was ten. As usual, I was at the airport and somewhere close to the hangar when a quick thundershower blew up. I was huddled against the wall and a man came along. It was a man I guess I had been watching and worshiping from afar for months.

"Come on in, kid, and keep dry," he said, pushing me toward the holy of holies, where the planes were kept. Inside, we talked all through the storm. That is, *he* talked and I said "Yessir" and "Nosir" every once in a while. Then the rain stopped and we started to go out.

"Thanks a lot, sir," I said.

"That's fine, kid," said my benefactor. "Say, you think a lot of flying, don't you? Like to take a flip someday?"

Would I! Okay. Go home and ask your mother, if she says it's all right, I'll take you for a ride. Can you picture the ten-year-old who rode the trolley back to Montreal and on down into Verdun, the suburb where home was?

The family thought it was just a gag. Who'd take a ten-year-old sky-riding? Sure, you can fly, mom said. Sure, you can go to the moon!

I was back at Cartierville the next morning, long before the planes were out on the apron, looking for my pilot. "Mister! Mister!" I began to yell when he was still fifty yards away. "It's all right. I can go. My mom says I can fly!"

"All right, son, all right," the man said. "Keep your shirt on. We'll fly . . . right now, if you like!"

Ten minutes later we were in the air, heading toward the mountain and the city . . . and I was a flier for the rest of time, no matter what happened. From now on the world would never be the same again!

The man I rode out and up with that morning remains my best friend and adviser to this day. Bush pilot, barnstormer, instructor, and now parachute tester, Ted Hogan is the fellow who brought me along, who found odd jobs for me to do around the Cartierville field and who, by the time I was twelve, was letting me get the feel of the controls. Mom thought I ought to be a doctor. Dad hoped I would become a commercial artist. But Hogan always said: "Fly, kid. It's the only life!" It sure is!

By the time I was fourteen I was selling papers and magazines, building model aircraft and selling them to the other kids around Verdun, running errands, doing anything I could find time to do to scrape money together for flying lessons. Whenever he could find the time Ted would take me up and let me fly his Rambler around, always for free. Not once did he accept a cent from me. It used to take about a month to earn $10 and whenever that total had been reached I'd quit everything else to plunk my big bill down on the counter and buy an hour's dual from one of the other instructors, usually a chap named Champagne, whom everybody called "Fizzy." Finally, when I was sixteen, my dad helped out with the last wad of bills to let me finish my dual and start out on my own. I was away!

If you've come straight from school, factory, or office to the Air Force, your first solo is liable to be an occasion preceded by something closely resembling the jitters, I guess. But if you've been hanging around airdromes since you were nine and have spent the last couple of years running errands and washing down planes to earn money for flying lessons, it's your real big moment. Mine was, anyway. I did two circuits and landings, and they were *good* landings. I can still feel those skis touching snow, soft as feathers, for the great day happened in midwinter. You have to give some of the credit to the skis and the snow-covered field, because the combination gives better take-offs and smoother landings than wheels and hard ground. Even so, they were good landings, and I felt swell.

In the air I was tempted to chuck the little Rambler about, as Ted used to let me when we were up together and I had the controls. But I wanted to keep on flying, not to be grounded as a smart aleck on my first solo. So the Rambler and I were very dignified as we swept around the field and landed.

Aerobatics were strictly out at Cartierville in 1938. This was a purely commercial school, the purpose of which was to enable youngsters to learn the rudiments of flight, and nobody wanted any Ramblers washed out by would-be aces. I soon found that out, for on my fourth flip, after a total solo flying time of an hour and a half, I did my first bit of unorthodox flying, yanking the stick hard back and kicking on full rudder to throw the little crate over in a flick roll, which is neither more nor less than a horizontal spin. Unfortunately for me, I selected a spot immediately over the field for this escapade. It came off beautifully and I flew around Cartierville feeling like a king. The feeling didn't last long. When I landed and taxied up to the hangar Mike Beaudoin, one of the school's instructors, was waiting for me.

"What the hell do you think you're doing with that ship?" he barked, before I had climbed out of the cockpit. "Any more of that and you're out, so far as this joint is concerned. Don't you go trying things you're not capable of doing, not with *our* ships!"

Just exactly how a guy was ever going to become a pilot by flying around like a truck driver, I didn't know. But for once I kept my trap shut. From then on I made plenty sure I was out of sight of the airport before attempting any aerobatics, though I'd done practically everything in the book while flying with Ted Hogan, dual.

Mostly I'd sneak off in the general direction of Dorval, where Montreal's new passenger and Atlantic Ferry airport has since been built, to do my stuff. Seems to me the next item I added to my repertory was a spin. Taking the Rambler up to 2,500 feet, out over Lake St. Louis, I closed the throttle and started to ease the control column back. As the nose came up over the horizon and the flying speed began to fall away to almost nothing, I kicked on right rudder and over we fell, spinning to the right. I let her spin down to about 1,000 feet, then centered the controls and waited for her to make her way out. The Rambler was pretty slow about it, so to help her along I gave her a bit of opposite rudder, and out she came. I was beginning to feel like a great pilot already.

My first loop was something else, because a lap-belt is nothing to hang by when you're over on your back and you either loop a Rambler right, or you hang there until she makes up her mind to fall out of the loop, or *you* fall out of the cockpit! So I fussed around quite a while before I screwed up the courage to do what I'd promised myself. At last, however, I shoved the nose down and dived until I had built up a speed of 160 miles an hour. Then I yanked the stick back into my stomach and around we went, the old crate creaking and groaning like a schooner in a gale. What a difference between the school ships of '38 and today's Spitfire! If you're cruising a Spit at 300 miles an hour all you do to loop is to ease the stick back gently—and I mean *gently*—a couple of inches, and over she goes.

Where to find money to lay on the line at $10 an hour for solo time was the big problem all that winter, and I was a young man in a hurry. Someplace I'd heard that the Chinese sorely needed pilots in their war with the Japs, that we pretended we hadn't heard about, and I was determined to get there somehow. First, however, I had to make a pilot of myself. That took time, plus money I didn't have. I took the problem home and told mother and dad that I wanted to quit school and take a job to earn enough money to qualify for my private pilot's certificate. I didn't mention China. Mother and dad are certainly not the kind of people who would have looked with favor on the idea of their son horning into "somebody else's war." But they knew I was determined to be a flier. So they said okay.

I found a job in the RCA-Victor radio plant at 28 cents an hour and rented a room near the factory for $1.50 a week. I'd spend another $1.75 a week on food, grabbing a cup of coffee and a hot dog here, a glass of milk and a piece of pie there, and cut every other expense to the bone, to scratch together a $10 bill every week for an hour alone in the air. In my own thoughts, at least, I was already on my way to China.

Once a week I'd turn up at Cartierville with my $10 in my hand and lay my money on the line, get a ship and, telling the school I was going to fly cross-country, would beetle off over the open fields, miles away from the drome, and put the Rambler through her paces. But that isn't all I did. Every now and then I'd pick up an extra hour in exchange for odd jobs around the school—washing down aircraft and doing chores around the hangar. Scarcely a day passed which didn't see me at Cartierville as soon as I could get away from the factory and usually there'd be something to do that could be traded into flying time. Trust Ted Hogan for that!

One by one I tackled all the standard aerobatics: sideslips, falling leaves, stall and Immelmann turns, and finally, the slow roll, a tricky number to execute with an old crate. I won't forget that first slow roll if I live to be a hundred. I went into it pleasantly enough, diving the Rambler to about 115 miles an hour, at which speed she'd begin to hum like a mouth organ, before easing the stick back and lifting the nose slightly above the horizon, controls centered. Then I put on vertical bank and top rudder, to get over on my back. That's where things began to go wrong. At this juncture the next step (if you know how to roll and keep your wits about you) is to put on a bit of opposite rudder and ease the stick back slightly, though still holding it in the banking position. Keep it there, but center it and center the rudder bar, and out you'll roll. What happened to me, God only knows. I imagine I applied wrong rudder, neglecting to remember that the controls become temporarily reversed when the ship is upside down. Whatever it was, I waddled and barrel-rolled out like a fat woman skidding round a corner. For the first time I felt completely disconcerted in the air. So I stayed out over the farming country west of Montreal and did more rolls, until I mastered them and had my confidence back.

I kept my job in the radio plant until the end of February, 1939, but wasn't at all happy about things. One week's work, no matter how close I cut corners on food, room and laundry, gave me just enough cash for an hour's flying. Even though I was picking up extra time on the trade-in system I'd be an old man before I qualified for my ticket, and there was no point in starting for China without one. I took my problem, as usual, to Ted Hogan, the only friend I had who seemed to know what I had on my mind and to accept it as reasonable.

"What you ought to do," he said, "is to get in with some small commercial outfit, somebody freighting supplies north to the mining camps, or to fur traders, or something like that, and get them to take you on. Maybe I can dig up something. Hold your horses a few days."

A week later Ted asked me: "Ever hear of a place called Gravenhurst, up in Ontario, north of Toronto?"

I said no, I hadn't. Why?

"There's a guy up there," Hogan said, "name of Smith Langley, who has a Curtiss Robin and some kind of freighting contract into the Rouyn goldfields. They tell me he could use a little help."

"I'm on my way," I said.

"How you going to get there?" Ted wanted to know. "Need a little dough?"

I said no, I'd be okay. Ride the rods. That night I checked out of my room and sent a message around to the plant that I was quitting, said good-bye to the folks . . . and started for China, via Gravenhurst, Ontario.

Toronto was reached in modest comfort in an empty freight car, without incident. From there I thumbed rides north and, three days out of Montreal, hit Gravenhurst and found Langley. We struck a deal without trouble. What he needed was help; what I needed was flying time. We traded even, with grub and bunk thrown in. I stayed about six weeks, during which we slammed the Robin up and down the Gravenhurst-Rouyn run, day in and day out, hustling to complete a contract job before the ice went out of the northern lakes and left us shy on landing fields. Thanks to Langley I put in enough time to qualify for my permit, equivalent of the private license. That happened on April 16th. Langley's Gravenhurst job was finished, so I hoicked back to Toronto and began to hunt westbound transportation in the freight yards.

Twelve days passed as I rode the rods from Toronto to Merrit, British Columbia, where my great-uncle George, a well-known surgeon, lived. En route I traveled in at least forty freight trains, had the odd skirmish with the railway police in Toronto and Winnipeg, but finally made it. Mostly the train crews were good fellows and not too hard on riders, unless the cops were around.

As soon as I told my uncle what I had on my mind he wanted to help me. I said I couldn't think of a thing; everything seemed to be going along all right. But next morning, at breakfast, he passed an envelope across the table. "If you're going to China," he said, "maybe this will help." Into the envelope he had tucked a check for $500. God bless my only rich relative!

Uncle George's gift put a new complexion on my travels. Now I had money in my jeans to put in enough flying time to really make a pilot of myself. That day I boarded a passenger train for Vancouver and headed out to Sea Island Airport, plunked my cash down on the counter; I paid for fifty hours in advance and went to work to polish up my aerobatics. That was early in May, 1939.

Len Foggen's school at Sea Island was equipped with a couple of Luscombes, a Bird, and a Fleet, all good, tough little trainers, and on them I went about the business of learning to throw an airplane around the sky, at the end of which time I passed the written and flying examinations for my commercial ticket, only to learn that I was too young to be licensed. While I was waiting for the bad news on the exams, I put in another seventy hours flying passengers around the drome for Foggen, just to pile up the logbook entries. I figured now that I was all set for China, with or without a commercial license, and set out again on my Odyssey.

One night late in July I rode an eastbound freight out of the Vancouver yards, leaving it near Soumas, where I crossed the United States border on foot, on my way to San Francisco to look for a ship. In the very first town I hit, while lookii g for freight-car accommodation in the yards, I was accosted by a policeman. He wanted to know: "Where d'you come from, son, and where you heading for?" Like a sap I told the truth. The cop asked for my papers. I hadn't any. "Guess you and I better take a walk," he said.

That's as far as I ever traveled in the direction of China. Instead I languished in detention in Seattle for endless weeks while the American immigration authorities checked on me back home. At the end of the checkup I was shipped east with eight or nine other youngsters who had committed, like myself, the heinous crime of illegal entry. That sure made China a long way off. While I was crossing the continent, down in the mouth and wondering what to do next, Britain and Germany went to war. By the time I reached Montreal, Canada was on the point of jumping in. I began to take an interest in life again, sure that my own country would sign me on in a minute.

The folks were in something of a we-told-you-so humor. On the face of the evidence the prodigal had returned, broke, Uncle George's $500 scattered to the winds of Sea Island—and nothing to show for the money but a lot of "useless" flying time. The general suggestion seemed to be that I'd better forget about flying and get a respectable job for a change.

That was a perfectly sound point of view and only one factor prevented it becoming established policy— myself. Teams of wild horses couldn't have kept me away from airfields. There wasn't anything else I wanted. "Respectable" jobs on the ground appealed only as a means of earning money to spend on flying. I have a sneaking suspicion that everyone I knew, except Ted Hogan, regarded me as a glorious young pain in the neck about then. To my seniors I must have appeared as a young obsessed idiot who wouldn't listen to reason. But if I *had* listened, probably I'd be a full-fledged buck private in the Canadian Army by now, peeling potatoes in a cookhouse somewhere in England.

The first day home I set off, logbook in coat pocket, to enlist in the service of my country. The officer commanding the RCAF Recruiting Center in Montreal looked my papers over. We talked pleasantly for a while, but I could soon see I had embarked on another hopeless quest. In the first place, the RCAF didn't know what its war role would be. The big Training Plan hadn't emerged. Canada had practically no training aircraft and few fields. What capped the climax, however, was that even if they'd had everything, George Beurling still didn't have enough official book learning and not all the flying time in Christendom could qualify him for an aircrew job in the RCAF until he could meet the terms of the Regulations, or until the war became tough enough to be fought by people who weren't college men. I was a pretty bitter kid when I left the Recruiting Center. Here was the biggest flying show in man's history, just getting going, but your own country wouldn't even let you get into it! I left there convinced that flying experience, won the hard way, counted for nothing in this game any more. All that counted was a piece of paper saying you'd passed your algebra. Finding out that I couldn't fly for Canada was the toughest blow of the lot.

Two or three days later, out at Cartierville, I heard that the Finns were recruiting fliers and would take anybody with a pilot's license. I didn't waste a minute. Hotfoot I raced into the city to offer my services. The consul looked through my logbook, talked to me about his country, and wound up by telling me they'd be more than glad to have me. Only one trick remained before we could rack up the hand. As I was still a minor, the consul would have to drop a note to dad, just to secure his formal permission. The way the old boy said it, however, convinced me that to call it a formality was to exaggerate. Obviously my father would be proud to have his son fly in the service of so gallant a people. I went home walking on air.

Then the letter came. Dad simply took one long look at its contents and asked: "What on earth's *this?*"

I told him that the whole thing was a mere formality. That's what the Finnish consul had called it. All dad needed to do was to sign his name on the dotted line, right there at the bottom of the page, and tomorrow morning I'd be in the employ of Finland.

Perfectly simple. "You *will* sign it, won't you?" I asked, pretty urgently, I imagine.

Dad simply looked up and said: "Nothing doing!" And that was that. No Finland for mè. In the light of what has happened since, both to Finland and to me, it was probably a wise decision. But as it looked at the time it was just another of those grown-up whimseys, designed to keep a youngster from doing the one job he *knew* he could do well. If you had described my condition as broken-hearted about then you would have been putting it mildly. No China. No Finland. Even Canada seemed to want no part of me.

On the last score, dad thought maybe we could do something and promised to go around to the Recruiting Center with me and see if he couldn't help me talk my way in. Here, at least, was a thread of hope to grasp. But the thread soon broke. A squadron leader interviewed us and the whole tone of what he said could be summed up in the phrase "Too bad!" The Regulations were there. He hadn't written them, but he did have to follow them. The fact that I had better than 150 flying hours solo didn't make the slightest difference. I lacked the educational qualifications called for by the Regs, and until I could meet those requirements I might just as well forget about the RCAF.

Right then I said the hell with it and got my job back at RCA-Victor, as unhappy a youngster as ever punched a time clock. As far as I was concerned I was done with flying—for all of twenty-four hours. Then I went in search of my pal Ted Hogan, for solace and advice.

"Look, kid," Ted said, "this thing is going to last a long time and everybody in the world is going to get a crack at it, one way and another, before it's over. The way I figure, it's the real Big Show this time, and it's going to have a long run. Before we're done this country will need every flier it can find and train. So will the United States. So will England. So will everybody. If the Air Force setup looks screwy to you, just remember those guys and the government weren't ready for this, any more than England was or America will be when her turn comes. Just hold your fire, kid. You'll get your chance, don't worry. Meanwhile, if you feel like it"—and here Ted pasted me a real old clap on the back—"we might take a few flips and see if there's anything on your list that needs polishing up!"

God bless that guy Hogan! I think he kept me alive, that first winter of the war. He flew with me, always encouraging me, and he ironed the rough spots out of my flying. He made me bone up on my unfinished high school courses and he dug up textbooks on all manner of aviation subjects, plowing knowledge into my skull that soon would be invaluable to me. Somehow the winter wore along. By spring I had 250 hours solo and had become a pretty good flier, or as good as I could get to be on the only crates I could find to fly. Then along in May, 1940, I was grounded by the Cartierville people for low-stunting, and found myself facing a month during which I wouldn't be allowed to leave the ground. That left plenty of time for brooding. I guess everything looked like plain persecution to me.

Sometime while the month was wearing along, while wandering around the business district, I met a lad I knew who clerked for a shipping firm. Like most guys of my acquaintance, he was inclined to rib me about my determination to go overseas as a pilot. My line had worn threadbare, I guess. Even my pals thought I was kidding.

"Look, George," he said, "if you're so anxious to get over there, why don't you just pack up and go?"

"I don't get you," I answered. "What does a guy use for money?"

"Hell," said my friend, "you don't need money. Work your way over on a freighter!"

"Swell," I said skeptically. "How does a person who doesn't know one end of a ship from the other get himself a job on one?"

According to this lad, it was as simple as wink. Practically every ship to make port was shorthanded and looking for men. All you had to do was to go down to the docks, cross the gangplank of the first ship you saw, and sign on. If that was true, I'd certainly been missing plenty of tricks.

"Nothing to it," my friend went on. "You take today. Our company are agents for a ship called the *Valparaiso* that is loaded with munitions and all set to go. The captain's been looking all over town for men!"

"You mean she's sailing right away?"

"In about an hour. I just came from there."

"Listen," I said, "where do I find this *Valparaiso?*"

My friend told me. Such-and-such a berth. A motor ship. A Swede.

"Fine," I said, suddenly feeling alive again, after months of frustration. "Now, listen, Jack. I'm going to run like hell to my boardinghouse and get my other shirt. Give me two days. If you don't hear from me by then, you'll know I made it, so go round and tell the folks where I've gone."

Forty-five minutes later I walked up the *Valparaiso's* gangplank and shipped for the round trip as a deckhand!

The ship, loaded with shells, steamed down the St. Lawrence and into an east coast port, where we rode at anchor for several days until our convoy was assembled and ready to sail. All told, seventy merchantmen formed up in lines astern, with naval escort out on the flanks. For eighteen days we wallowed up hill and down dale while a would-be fighter pilot

scrubbed decks, chipped paint, took a turn as helms-
man, and generally made himself useful, four hours
out of each twelve. The crew were swell guys. God
knows how they can take it the way they do, month in
and month out, having ships knocked out from under
their feet, getting back to shore if they're lucky,
shipping again with the next convoy. That takes guts,
that does! Just think of the infinite number of things
that can happen to you: torpedoes, mines, surface
raiders, bombs; storms to knock you all over the ocean,
bum coal to make you fall out of convoy and be a soft
shot for any sub; gales to wash men overboard; you
can hit icebergs, submerged derelicts, or rocks near the
coast; if that isn't enough, the ship astern will probably crash into you during fog or darkness. Anything
can happen—anything unpleasant. A flier's lot is pie
by comparison with that of the merchant navy. Yet a
lot of smug people seem to want no part of the sailor
off a tanker or merchantman, because he comes ashore
in port in a peaked cap, with a dirty neck and no collar, heading for the nearest pub. He's the social or-
phan of the war and sometimes he gets to wondering
aloud, what in hell he's fighting for. I'm not surprised.
But I sure wish some of his so-called betters could hear
what the merchant navy thinks of *them*.

The crossing was rough but uneventful, until we
were approaching Ireland, when we walked head on
into one of Mr. Hitler's submarine packs. Before our

naval escort had things under control seven ships—
ten per cent of the convoy—had been torpedoed. It
all happened in ten minutes and ships were wallowing
in trouble, rolling over and diving for the bottom all
over the place, as the convoy scattered. The merchantmen didn't stop to pick up survivors. That was the

navy's job. We just got the hell out of there as fast as
our engines would take us, re-forming after the shin-
dig was over. Boy! Did I ever wish aloud to be riding
high in one of the big Sunderland boats that came
winging over us. The sea is not *my* element, that's
sure.

The rest of us made the Clyde right side up and
the *Valparaiso* tied up in Queen's Dock, Glasgow.
Now to find me a recruiting officer and sign up to fly.

I was flat broke, but managed to talk the captain into giving me an English pound against the $30 a month and $75 War Risk pay which would be coming to me at the end of the return trip I didn't intend to make. That would carry me until I hit an Air Force payday. Then I gathered my stuff together and sneaked across the gangplank, hoping nobody would see me carrying my satchel and know I was jumping ship. On the dock I met a policeman.

"How're you fixed for fliers over here?" I asked him.

In an accent I won't try to imitate he answered:

"By the look of things we need as bloody many as we can bloody well get!" That was my introduction not only to Scotland but to one of the two words used anywhere and everywhere by male residents of the island, between any two words in any sentence. I had arrived in what, since then, I've often heard called Great Bloody Britain!

The cop directed me to a recruiting station and I hoicked downtown on a streetcar, lighthearted as a fighting cock. "Half an hour more," I'd say to myself as the tram inched along the streets, "and I'll be in the RAF!" . . . "Twenty minutes more" . . . "Ten minutes more" . . . And so we came to the recruiting station.

A friendly flight lieutenant listened to my story.

"Splendid, splendid," he said. "Now let me see your papers."

I explained why I had none, that I'd left Montreal in a hell of a hurry, as the ship was on the point of sailing when I found it. If he'd take my word for it and sign me on, I'd be glad to send home for my logbook.

"Oh, it's not the logbook that worries me, old chap," he answered, "but your birth certificate. What about your birth certificate? Must have a birth certificate, you know, old man."

We must have talked about birth certificates for half an hour. But we were up against a brick wall. The flight lieutenant insisted I couldn't be taken on strength without one. I kept repeating that I'd never seen one in my life, but could probably get one sent over from home.

"Too bad, you know, old boy," the officer said finally, "but I'm afraid I'll have to ask you to go back and get it."

You'd think the Beurlings lived just across the street! But at least he wasn't worrying about my education. That was *something!*

That night I walked the streets of Glasgow, half tempted to join the army and let flying go to hell. But cripes! Probably I'd have to produce a birth certificate before they'd even let me peel potatoes. Is there some law which says nobody can shoot at a German until he has proved himself legitimate, or what?

By the time I had walked off this combination of rage and gloom it was midnight. By then I'd made up my mind. I'd show them. I'd ship home in the *Valparaiso* and bring those damned papers back to Britain if it was the last thing I did.

As we left the Clyde, German raiders bombed us. On our third day at sea we were struck a glancing blow by a torpedo. But somehow we limped across the Atlantic, up the St. Lawrence and into harbor at Montreal, which we reached on August 3rd. There I was paid off for the round trip, but signed on again and scurried home to get my logbook and a birth certificate.

When I walked in the door mother took one look at me and cried: "Why, George Beurling, where on earth have you been?" That night we held a family conference, and it was agreed at last that, inasmuch as I seemed to be determined to get into *somebody's* Air Force, the folks would give me any documents and signatures that might help. At least it would be something to know that the boy had settled down somewhere, even in the cockpit of a Spitfire! The four days ashore passed pleasantly. I hired a car and took mother for drives around the country, visited old friends and said good-byes. On the 8th the *Val* sailed again, her holds stuffed with explosives.

As before, we put in time getting to our convoy assembly point, waiting for other ships and generally getting organized. This time we were one of thirty ships, escorted by destroyers and flyingboats until we were well east of the North American coast. From there we sailed on alone until we were somewhere west of Ireland, where new naval and air escort picked us up to take us into the Clyde. The voyage was slow, but uneventful, though one of the Sunderlands sank a submarine as it lay in wait for the convoy in the Western Approaches. We pulled into Glasgow in the middle of a rousing air raid.

Then and there I jumped ship, this time for keeps, after talking the skipper into letting me have £15 in English money, practically all I had earned on the eastbound crossing. I grabbed my kit and made for shore. As I went down the gangplank the captain spotted me from the bridge-wing and yelled to a policeman on the dock: "Hold that man!" The bobby stopped me. It was the selfsame cop of whom I had asked directions on my last visit.

"Look," I said, "I've come over here to enlist in your Air Force. Are you going to stop me, just because the captain of a neutral ship tells you to? How do you know he isn't a Nazi sympathizer?"

The policeman stroked his chin and thought it over. "No," he said finally, "I'm bloody well not going to hurt you, Laddie! The hell with your bloody captain!"

Poor old *Valparaiso!* She got hers on her next eastbound trip, I heard. A lot of my pals went down with her.

The same officer was on duty at the recruiting station as last time. Do they never change shifts in Glasgow? I wondered. Are the same cops and the same recruiting officers always on duty?

"Well, here I am, sir," I said.

"I'll be damned!" the flight lieutenant exclaimed. "It's the Canadian again! Find your birth certificate all right?"

I laid the precious document on his desk and with it my logbook. The officer inspected the certificate closely, but showed no interest in the log until he had satisfied himself that I had been born. Then he apologized for "all the trouble" to which he had put me. "Not my fault, old boy," he explained. "Just the bloody Regs."

As soon as the facts of birth had been established beyond question, the RAF became my foster mother. The flying record still didn't seem to matter. In half an hour the British immigration authorities, at the flight lieutenant's suggestion, listened to what I had to say and gave me a landing certificate. Then the officer gave me a ticket to London and a chit to take to RAF headquarters in Adastral House. I reached London next morning as the district around Euston Station was being blitzed. Later that day, September 7, 1940, I signed articles to fly for King George, almost a year to the day from my arrival in Montreal from the expedition to China which had ended so ingloriously in the hoosegow in Seattle. I'd missed out on China's war. My own country hadn't been able to use me. I'd been yanked almost bodily out of Finland's flying corps. But at last I'd made it into the RAF and would wear the badge on which appears the Latin tag *Per ardua ad astra*. I'm no Latin scholar. The free translation will always be good enough for me—"To the Stars the Hard Way!"

CHAPTER II

The Pilot Learns To Fly

(ROBERTS: If young Beurling had been thinking that enlisting in the RAF meant that he would start flying again without further ado, he was in for a rude awakening. On the record, that is what he got. "My first discovery," he told me, "was that previous flying experience was rated at exactly zero. Believe me, I wasn't the only rookie pawing the ground with impatience, down at the Manning Depot. Before I'd been on the job a day I met another raw recruit with thousands of hours to his credit as an air-line pilot. Like everybody else he had to start out on the parade ground, then put in weeks at an Initial Training Wing, places where nobody ever gets more than one foot off the ground at a time. I hadn't been in the Air Force two days before I realized that I was still one hell of a long way from a Spitfire cockpit!"

The realization did something to the youngster. No wonder, considering the months of kicking around he had gone through to get in. But the corporals and the sergeants and the flight lieutenants couldn't be expected to know about that. Consequently, a certain justifiable amazement was to be discerned amongst commissioned and noncommissioned disciplinarians on being told, "I didn't come over here to stand at attention every time I ask somebody a question. I came over here to fly!" The simple logic of

32

such a point of view is irrefutable. But neither the officers nor the noncoms saw it in that light. They didn't debate the point. They simply slapped the young man down with CB every time he bobbed up with the observation, CB signifying confinement to barracks, which requires the confinee to drop in at the guardhouse every hour on the hour, after the day's work is done, and report his presence. The performance of menial, and often unpleasantly intimate, camp chores is an additional burden laid on those addicted to explaining their reasons for enlisting to their seniors. "But I soon learned," says George, "I learned that the kid with a chip on his shoulder is going to get it knocked off and that he can't beat the system. Once that begins to seep into your head you're learning the rudiments of discipline."

The winter of 1940-41, then, was not one of the happier periods of Beurling's life. Once the buffing job had been done by the drill sergeants of the Manning Depot the future Nazi-killer of Malta was shipped to Hendon Aerodrome, near London, as what he calls "chief chambermaid on the crash wagon" and put in a month polishing the brass-work of that utilitarian vehicle and filling German bomb craters on the field. "That's the damned English climate for you," was the explanation. "Rain and fog alternated for weeks. So the flying schools couldn't graduate their classes, which meant they couldn't take in new pupils. So everything backed up right to the source and we guys couldn't get into the Initial Training Wings to start our course. I was fit to be tied that fall."

Be that as it may, when the opportunity to take seven days' leave came at Hendon, Beurling elected to remain on the station and not spend it gallivanting up and down the West End of London, which is commonly regarded as par for young men far from home. Months had passed since he'd had the smell of motor oil in his nostrils. He certainly wasn't going to abandon the stench, just because the orderly room offered leave. Instead he hung around the drome and bummed passenger flips from Army Cooperation pilots, one of whom nearly destroyed the Beurling neck by attempting a forced landing on what turned out to be a swimming pool at Denham, England's Little Hollywood.

Christmas found Leading Aircraftman Beurling down in Devon on the threshold of his Initial Training Wing course at last. Holiday furlough was available, as school wouldn't assemble until the 29th, but he had no friends in England and decided he might just as well be in camp as on' his own in London. Christmas mail was still somewhere behind him, moving along from station to station. Few airmen remained in camp and he ate what he calls the "King's Dinner" in something resembling solitary state. The afternoon he spent on the cliffs, watching the seagulls.

"Now, there's something to see," he said, as we discussed the festive season. "The way a gull gets up on the step, like a seaplane, before taking off . . . the way he puts on just the right amount of bank for every turn . . . his technique as he glides down and always turns into the wind to land . . . Those perfect climbing turns he makes from his take-offs!"

Christmas with the gulls on the cliffs of Devon! Not one of the brighter Yuletides, even for a Rugged Individualist with his eyes on a Spitfire cockpit.

Initial Training Wing—ITW—gave him a new insight into the Royal Air Force and its people, for his classmates were Yanks, Canadians, South Americans, Australians, Rhodesians, South Africans, lads from India and from the Occupied Countries, as well as a healthy leaven of Englishmen. Many of them had worked their way from the far corners of the earth to join up and fly. Maybe it was there that the first feel of the team spirit began to touch him. These guys had something on their minds over and above the idea of flying for flying's sake. He'd better find out about it. It was a hard-working young aircraftman who boned up on Maths, Map Reading, Aircraft Recognition, Morse and the Aldis Lamp, Armament, Navigation, Meteorology and Airmanship that winter. And it was a lighthearted young aircraftman who, on April 18, 1941, received news of his posting to an Elementary Flying Training School—EFTS—in the Midlands. There would be escapades in the days ahead, but they'd be the escapades of a young hellion full of energy and the joy of flying, not the escapades of a kid with a chip on his shoulder.

At this juncture George sat bolt upright in his hospital bed, reached for his crutches and began to swing up and down the room like a nervous young race horse.

"Boy!" he exclaimed. "Was I ever rarin' to go when I saw those planes out in front of the hangars!")

Boy! Was I ever rarin' to go when I saw all those planes out in front of the hangars. Miles Magisters—that's Maggies from now on—cute as little brass buttons. I could hardly wait for that first flip.

I was allotted to a sergeant instructor called Sellers, a swell pilot who had been shot down in a Hurri-bomber during the Battle of Britain and the first boss I'd had in the RAF who showed any interest in my previous flying. Sellers looked my log over and said something about "Not much to teach you here!" and took me out for my first flip. When we were out on the far side of the drome and had turned the Maggie's nose into the wind he called, "Okay, Canada. Take her away!" Did I ever feel grand as we rolled across the field and took to the air! I hadn't touched the controls of an airplane since they'd grounded me the previous summer at Cartierville for low-flying.

We did three circuits and landings and as I gunned to take off for a fourth Sellers yelled: "The hell with this! Let's go take a look at England!" So we flew out into the back country, where I looped, rolled, and spun the Maggie while Sellers relaxed and let me have the sky to myself. I roamed around singing and whistling and laughing like a fool every time the little Maggie came about in a tight turn or twisted out of another spin. Cripes, I felt good!

Before my first solo I asked Sellers how about aerobatics and he said: "If you feel like it, go ahead.

But not over the drome, for God's sake, or they'll peel the hide off both of us." That sounded like Ted Hogan, back home in Cartierville. Before you knew it I was out of sight of the field and Maggie and I were trying our hand at slow rolls.

The days at Elementary School passed quickly. . . . Up with the lark when a corporal clattered through the students' sleeping quarters, banging on a garbage can and crying, "Wakee! Wakee!" (Who but an Englishman would dream up such a word?) . . . Then PT, breakfast, and down to the hangars for morning flying. If you flew in the morning, lectures occupied the afternoon. In the air pupils practiced instrument flying under the hood, cross-country flying and hedgehopping, forced landings and simple aerobatics. Dogfighting was out, unless instructors were along to pull ambitious pupils out of trouble, but every once in a while a couple of us would agree on a rendezvous, far away from home, and take a crack at each other. That way a fellow named Brown and I pretty nearly met our comeuppance, diving toward each other from positions about a mile apart at a height of 6,000 feet. Each held into his dive for the last split second. Then just as I ducked to go under Brownie, he ducked to go under me. In the nick of time one of us yanked his stick back and whipped over the other. Phew! I never had it closer with a Jerry at Malta. The two of us sneaked home hoping nobody from the school had been around the sky to see a couple of damfool pupils trying to kill each other.

Mostly I'd spend my solo flights putting into practice all the theoretical stuff I'd been sopping up from textbooks and working out on paper ever since leaving Canada. I spent hours practicing the trick of getting between other pilots and the sun, picking up the ground shadow of another guy's ship, and fiddling around above him until our two shadows merged. That meant I was directly between him and the sun and that just so long as I stayed there I had him at my mercy, unless I let somebody else play the same trick on me. From that vantage point I'd fool around over my victim, getting into good attack positions, or dodging in and out of clouds until I'd set up a buffet supper for myself. Invariably I'd be thinking in terms of deflection angles, although we had no equipment for sighting.

We had a lot of fun at EFTS. The instructors were all swell people who realized that a pilot's important job is to fly. If you were keen on flying, then you were an okay guy. If you weren't keen, not all the standing to attention in the world would be worth a damn to you. I'd teamed up with a couple of English fellows, Bob Seed and Paul Forster, and we'd hell around the sky together, getting in and out of our spots of trouble, none of it serious—things like "shooting up" near-by villages, diving on them and prac-

WHEN I CAME BACK THE CHIEF FLYING INSTRUCTOR HAULED
ME UP ON THE CARPET AND GAVE ME MERRY HELL

ticing machine-gunning the populace with guns you didn't have. That would stir up civilian tempers a bit. The mayor would ring up the station to complain and the CO would give the whole school a public bawling-out as a matter of routine, and that would be that. Other times we'd dive on cattle in the fields and the farmer would yell ruddy murder about it on the phone, telling the adjutant we were souring his milk, or something. Once in a while we'd come down low over workmen in the fields or on the roads, then pull up suddenly and blow their caps off with our slip-streams. You can imagine what a popular bunch of guys we were. But I only got into one jackpot at Elementary School and it wasn't so bad.

A bunch of us were out in front of the hangar and I was just getting ready to climb into the cockpit of a Maggie when Bob, or Paul, or some other lame-brain, said: "I double-dare you to zoom up the side of the control tower." "It's a bet," I said and taxied out. On the take-off I lifted the Mag until I suppose we were about ten feet off the grasstops, then held her nose down and roared across the field head on at the tower. Just as I came up close I slammed the stick back and up we went, like climbing a wall. As I whisked past I saw a guy on the gallery dive over the railing for the roof of a hangar, ten feet below him. It was the sentry. He went one way, his rifle the other.

When I came back I found out just what I'd

done. The sentry had gone over the fence, diving, and hadn't fared too well when he hit the roof, which apparently didn't give much when he landed. The poor bloke, in addition to being scared grayheaded, had picked up an assortment of cuts and bruises that he was nursing for a week. All this I heard from the chief flying instructor, who hauled me up on the carpet and gave me merry hell. But there was a twinkle in his eye when he bawled me out that made me feel easier. I'd expected to be grounded—and wouldn't that have been something for guys like Seed and Forster to laugh about. I could even picture them visiting me in the cookhouse and giving me brotherly advice on how to peel potatoes, or empty the slop buckets.

By mid-June I'd done my fifty hours Elementary and was given seven days' leave before moving on to Service School. Right then one of the most pleasant things happened to me of all my experiences in Britain. We had an officer on the station, a middle-aged chap named Webb who was always more than decent to the kids who had come from all over the world to fly for the RAF.

"Where are you spending your leave, Canada?" Webb asked. I said I hadn't the slightest idea. No plans. Probably London.

"If you like the country," he said, with that half-shy manner so many of the good Englishmen have, as if they felt they weren't quite minding their own business, "I'd love to take you down to my little place in Wales, in the mountains near Chirk. Ever hear of Chirk?"

I said no, I hadn't, but I'd like to come, if it wouldn't be a nuisance to him. (Jiminy! I thought. I'm getting as polite as these educated Englishmen myself.) So to Chirk I went, to discover, of all things, that my host's peacetime occupation was estate manager, or something of the sort, for Lord Howard de Waldron. I had seven swell days down in the mountains of Wales, climbing them, shooting rabbits, and roaming around the old moated castle, with its torture chamber to remind you of the kind of wars people used to get themselves into before Spitfires were designed, when the can opener was mightier than the sword. But more important than the castle or the mountains was the idea of living in a real house, a home, for a few days. Believe me, that's the sort of thing a guy appreciates when he's halfway around the world from where he belongs, even if he is a roamer.

If the British want to get anything out of this war they ought to toss in a couple of colonies and ask for a piece of California, for if the sun never sets on their empire, it seldom rises over the main island. The gluey weather was at work as usual when we finished at Elementary, so we had to stall around again for a couple of weeks, waiting for courses ahead of us at the

Service School to graduate and get out of the way. So Bob and Paul and I were shipped off to a drome down near Peterborough to fly Moths and wait. It rained there too.

We checked in at our new home, not far from Montrose, up in Scotland, on June 23rd to find Bill Allen, of Montreal, who had been my sidekick at ITW already on deck. That made the threesome a foursome. We began to fly right away, dual, on Miles Masters, a two-place plywood job probably best described as a two-seater Hurricane. The Hurries came later. The Master is a little honey to fly. Takes off fast and lands fast, but when you actually come down to it, just another pair of wings with an engine and a fuselage. Some of the boys pranged a few, but the only fatal crackup of the course, on the two-seaters, came when three ships, practicing turns in formation, tangled and took fire in the air, killing three instructors and two pupils, the third pupil baling. But that wasn't the fault of the aircraft. Somebody got the jitters, or didn't keep his eyes peeled for that other wingtip. Eight times out of ten when something like that goes wrong you get the same answer—Pilot Error. I know that's what got me into nearly every flying jam I ever walked into—that little lapse on my own part that can make the difference between flying tomorrow and never flying again.

Night flying, formation flying, cross-country, instrument flying, aerobatics, low-flying and practice attacks on ground targets (but not cows, and not farmers in the fields) occupied our time at Service Flying Training School—SFTS—and still no dog-fighting allowed. The two and a half months on that Scottish station were a lot of fun. You knew you were going places at last. But it sure takes time.

Trouble? Not in the ordinary sense of the word. Call it fun. Like the time I played alarm clock for Charlie Chambers . . .

Chambers was an English lad, married and allowed a sleeping-out pass, which permitted him to board with his wife at a farmhouse near the drome. Well, Chambers came to me one night and said:

"You on early flying tomorrow, Beurling?"

I said yes, I was.

"Do me a favor," he said. "Be a good fellow and wake me up, will you?"

I said I would.

So next morning I was over Chambers's farm-house about 7:30 around 2,000 feet, all set to call Charlie. From there I went down in a vertical dive, full throttle and fully-fine pitch, roaring like seventeen kinds of bedlam. I held the Master in its dive until it was a case of pull out or go in through the roof and out the Chambers's bedroom window, swinging up and away just in time to spot Trouble hanging right on my tail. Trouble was another aircraft, which I recognized by its markings as that of Wing Commander McKenna, the chief flying instructor on our drome. So help me, the CFI had followed me down to see what I was up to!

I banked away smartly to try and hide the numbers on my own plane and the wingco began chasing me around the sky like a speed cop. For a while I got around on his tail. He'd never see my markings as long as I could stay there. But the wing commander was no fellow to let a young pup ride him for long. First thing you knew he was on *my* tail. I wriggled loose and made a break for it and he chased me all round the Grampian Mountains for at least half an hour. Finally McKenna had to turn back home, or run out of gas, and he left me. I swung around in a tremendous half circle and tried to sneak back into the field innocently, as if I'd been off south somewhere. That helped a lot—I *don't* think! Before I could climb out of the cockpit the flight sergeant was right there beside me, with something of a glint in his eye as he said:

"Wing Commander McKenna wants to see you right away, Beurling!"

Oh-oh.

"Young man," the CFI said, "exactly what in hell were you doing, diving on that farmhouse at half past seven? Trying to frighten the farmer's daughters out of their nightshirts?"

I thought fast and looked innocent, I hoped.

"Sir," I answered, always the well-disciplined airman, "I saw something flash on the ground and thought maybe somebody had hit the deck. So I went down to investigate, according to orders!"

The winco looked at me sternly for a minute, then grinned.

"All I can say, Beurling," he said, "is that I never saw a quicker ruddy investigation in my life. Carry on, then. You ought to do very well in this business."

Not what you'd call trouble, exactly. Just one of those unfortunate accidents.

(ROBERTS: "And the rest of the time," I said, "you were the essence of maidenly decorum. Right?"

"Whatever that is," said George. "Oh, shucks, I was on the spot a couple of times for missing the odd lecture. That happens to everybody. But no trouble, no crime-sheet stuff."

Suddenly he grinned from ear to ear. "Cripes!" he said. "There was one little affair. But nothing came of it."

"Tell me," I said.

Well, there was this sergeant, who'd been ground crew and had remustered to train as a pilot. That meant he kept his stripes, whereas everybody else was plain air-craftman, which is just about buck private. The sergeant liked that. Gave him an edge, and he was that kind of guy. Used to march all the other students to and from the hangar and to and from classes. Everybody got sort of sick of it. So one day young Beurling spoke the public mind, out loud. "For a pupil like the rest of us, you're too damned fond of giving orders!" This statement of fact, though eminently pleasing to his fellows, was not well received by the gentleman for whom it was intended, and George was asked to drop in and see the station commander . . . but fast! The incident was adjusted by a fatherly homily from the group captain, more or less on the basis of go-and-sin-no-more. George left the orderly room smarting with a sense of grievance and proposing to square accounts.

Somewhere in the hut-lines that night he found the sergeant and invited the three-striper to put up his dukes and "go to town." The sergeant demurred, but Beurling was obdurate, to the point of pasting him in the nose, by way of getting things started. After that the two young men slugged it out for several minutes, while Seed, Forster, and Allen stood guard at the ends of the hut. That brought George right back to the starting point, the carpet in front of the CO's desk.

"In God's name, man!" the group captain barked. "What are you doing around here, running a private war of your own? I can't spend my time criming people all over the place. That's not what you're here for. But I can't let you go around blacking sergeants' eyes, even if they are students, like yourself. Now what have you got to say about this mess?"

"Well," said George, "I did a little quick thinking and came up with the suggestion that there must be a mistake somewhere. I guess I sort of suggested that the sergeant must have walked into a door, or the corner of a hut, in the blackout, possibly on his way home from the wet canteen, which could explain the black eye. Far as I was concerned, I'd spent the evening in my quarters, studying, and would be glad to bring witnesses to prove it. Hell, the whole outfit would have sworn black was white to give that guy a trimming!"

The CO must have been slightly taken aback by this

insouciant explanation, or perhaps he was simply a very wise person. In any event he dismissed the case for lack of evidence. Later he met the hero of the incident in the vicinity of one of the hangars and, returning the young man's salute, stopped him. "You know, Beurling," he said, "there's something I thought of saying to you this morning, but the time didn't seem quite right. If I were you, I'd save some of that unbounded energy of yours for the Germans. You may need it someday."

"Great guy!" grinned Beurling. "Certainly knew the score.")

Everything went along smooth as silk until we began to fly Hurricanes, along toward the end of the course. Oh, a few guys pranged the two-seaters in the ordinary course of events, but nothing serious, apart from that one bad mess-up on the formation job. The Hurries took quite a toll, however, You have to expect these things. You can't train fighter pilots on kiddie-cars.

The commander of the Hurricane Flight was Flying Officer Upton, D.F.C., a Canadian who had bagged nine Huns in the Battle of Britain, not only a swell fellow, but a grand instructor. No cinch job, teaching people what to do before they take their first flip in a single-seater. That's a big moment in any young pilot's life, and he's liable to be pretty jittery. But Upton handed out the sort of cockpit drill which gave people confidence in themselves and tipped them off to all the Hurri's little tricks. They're swell babies to fly, but light as a feather on the ailerons and will roll just by putting the pressure of a finger on the controls. Their trickiest spot is near the ground, for the Hurri tends to drop a wing as she comes in and you can swipe the undercart off her and ground-loop quick as winking. But Upton would mother every pupil along, giving him plenty of cockpit rehearsals, then, when the big moment came, clap the lad on the back and say: "Remember, now, old fellow, don't pull up the undercart until you're well airborne. Good luck. Away you go!" Then he'd stand back and sweat while he watched another fighter-pilot-in-the-making solo. There was one lad on our course I remember particularly for his first Hurricane flip. For some reason or other his undercarriage jammed and the poor kid was floa ing around the drome, trying to get the lever to work, without luck. Upton promptly took off in another machine and flew alongside the boy for ten minutes or so, giving him all kinds of fatherly advice. No dice. The undercarriage remained re-tracted. Finally Upton came down, ordered the crash wagon out and fired green lights, the signal to the kid to come in for a crash landing. The boy did, but in the excitement forgot to lower his flaps and came tearing across the drome at about a hundred miles an hour. He hit on his belly and jumped and slewed around until the Hurri ultimately came to rest, a complete write-off. The pilot stepped out of the cockpit—with a sprained wrist!

Upton's luck, like that of so many grand pilots, ran out in the end. From Scotland he came back to Canada on leave, but returned to Britain to instruct on Spitfires. He was killed while dogfighting with a pupil. Knowing your stuff isn't enough in itself in the fighter business. You have to have your luck with you too.

Our days on Hurricanes at SFTS were not without tragedy, and not without laughs. On the tragic side we lost a couple of Polish fellows—Boy, do those guys ever hate the Germans!—who collided while flying side by side and crashed into the sea. Another Pole—there were a lot of them around the schools in '41—got caught over the water with an overheated engine and baled. He pulled his ripcord too soon after leaving the cockpit and it caught on the aircraft. He went down into the sea like a plummet. Then there was another lad who, after overshooting the drome, gunned to go around again but got caught with a sputtering engine which died on him completely as he was turning to come back to the field. He tried to stretch his glide to reach the drome and, as so often happens when the glide is cut fine, stalled and spun. He almost pulled out, but hit the water. All we ever saw of him was an oil patch where he went in.

On the lighter side was the case of Chuck Gardner, a Scot, who went wandering away up near Aberdeen without remembering to switch over to his main fuel tank. Chuck's engine died and his prop stopped. Still he forgot to switch tanks and began to arrange his affairs for a forced landing. He picked a field and hit the near fence going so fast the Hurri took off by itself and jumped three fields in pieces. Chuck told us later that wings and all manner of chunks of Hurricane were flying in every direction. The cockpit and center section took off on its own and landed intact. Chuck simply unstrapped himself, stepped out, and went in search of a telephone. A strange business, this.

My only mishaps were minor, one a wheels-up landing on a Master while flying dual with an instructor, shortly after my arrival in Scotland; the other a precautionary landing, also on a Master, but solo, the result of undercarriage trouble. On the Hurries my luck was fine. I spent my last three weeks in Scotland on them and left for Operations Training with the feeling that I knew something about single-seaters. For the first time in my life I had ridden downhill at better than 500 miles an hour, the speed and resistance ripping the fabric off the sealed gunports. I'd chucked 'em about and split-assed all over the Scottish sky. I sure was beginning to look forward to those Spitfires.

On September 7, 1941, school broke up. There was no graduation ceremony, no Wings Parade, no fuss. You simply went and bought yourself a pair of wings and a set of sergeant's stripes and put 'em up. Bob and Paul were commissioned on graduation, Bill and I were simple sergeant pilots—just a couple of undisciplined colonials, I guess. In my logbook for that day there is an entry signed by Squadron Leader Slater, who had instructed me on Masters.

"To be useful as a Service Pilot," the notation reads, "he should cultivate a sense of responsibility."

CHAPTER III

Prepare for Action!

THE instructors at the Operational Training
Unit, to which we reported for the final stage of pre-
combat flying, were an all-star aggregation, mostly
members of the few to whom the many owe so much—
the birds who flew the Battle of Britain. Topnotcher,
beyond question, was Flight Lieutenant Ginger Lacey,
D.F.M. and Bar, with twenty-five German Aircraft
Destroyed to his credit as a sergeant pilot from the
Big Blitz and the pre-Dunkirk days across the
Channel. Lacey is the lad who shot down the Heinkel
which bombed Buckingham Palace and was himself
shot down by the Jerry rear-gunner, baling down into
the garden of the palace, where he was kept for
tea by the King and Queen. The others—Baroldi,
Powling, Wade, the whole tribe—were out of the same
RAF top drawer. The place was stiff with medal rib-
bons, and if you'd added up the sum total of Huns
Destroyed represented by the staff of the station, it
would have run into the hundreds. That, in itself,

was a thrill for the freshmen pilots whom these warriors would groom for battle. At OTU you felt as if you had one foot in the door at last.

For the first time since we had reported to our Elementary Flying Schools and soloed on Maggies, the lid was off. Up to now, training had been based on the idea of what the student was ready for: Could he be trusted in formation, in aerobatics, in dog-fighting? Had he enough flying experience for this-and-that? Had he proved himself temperamentally suited for a fighter pilot's job? Now it was the other way around. You'd earned your wings. You'd shown you had the stuff in you. You'd tossed Hurricanes around the sky. Okay. Give the kid a Spitfire and let him go to town. When he leaves here he's got to be ready to knock Huns down. So he'd better be good!

I'd come down to OTU from seven days' leave in London and for the first time I can remember I was plain, redheaded mad with the whole damned German race. I'd seen things during that week, the sort of things I'd looked at before in pictures, but not close at hand in the flesh. Sure, I'd seen bombs fall in Glasgow, and I'd been in London before when the Jerries came over, and camps I'd been in had been bombed. But those shows had seemed more like larks. Now, somehow, it was different.

One of those days I was in Tottenham Court Road when the Huns lifted the tailboard and let go everything they had, and there'd been a little bit of a girl sitting on the curb, playing with a doll. A policeman and I had seen her at the same time and had run over to her, because she didn't even seem to know the raid was going on. As I got there the bobby was saying, "Better run along, baby. It's too dangerous to be playing here!" Then we both saw. The child was alive all right. But she was stunned, or in a stupor, just sitting there looking at her unhurt doll—her own right arm blown clean off at the shoulder!

Or what about that other day, when the raiders caught me sitting in the window of the Canadian Legion Club, watching the world go by—and, if you want to know it, watching one of the prettiest girls I ever laid eyes on going up the street in a hurry, for the sirens were blowing. Right then the stuff began to hit and three or four minutes later somebody rushed into the club to say a big one had dropped spang on the shelter, just up the street. We all hoicked over, to lend a hand. Debris had blocked the shelter entry and a German bomb had burst the water main in the street. We started pulling stuff out of the way and people came pouring out. But there was one person who couldn't. She was pinioned there by a huge dislodged stone that a dozen men couldn't budge, and the water from the broken main was pouring around her and rapidly filling the ruins of the shelter. From somewhere a surgeon arrived. Without a moment's delay he went to work. Anaesthetic and amputation kit—and he took off at the thigh the leg pinned under that huge slab of rock, to save its owner from death by drowning. It was the same pretty girl I'd watched tripping by the Legion Club not an hour before!

For me, from that day forward, I say God damn the Germans, the whole kit and caboodle of those who march with their bastard leaders and those who accept such leadership because they haven't the guts to die bucking it! That's tough talk. Roberts says maybe I'm oversimplifying the problem. Well, maybe. I kind of have a hunch it's the way the Russkies feel too, and a lot of ordinary guys in England. *And* the Maltese. There's only 250,000 of them. But believe me they're not feeling friendly to the Huns, or to the Eyeties either. Would you, if your home town had been knocked cockeyed, and all your kids were either dead or crippled? Hell, I better go hire a hall! But that's the way I felt, after seeing that little baby and her doll, and that wonderful-looking girl in the bombed-in shelter! I began to feel ashamed that up to now I'd been thinking of this air war as nothing but a great adventure for those who can fly.

You can't afford to be one of these hot-blood haters in this game, though. Many a good guy I know has gone west because he felt so violent about Germans and so damned anxious to pot the one in his sights that he forgot about the Hun on his own tail. It's a cold-blooded business. And it's a cold-blooded job we've got to do on the swine.

That's the mood I was in when I taxied out to the Operational Training Unit from the station and seven days in blitzed London. Give me a Spitfire! Let me get going! Then I got down to the job of making a combat flier, a fighter pilot, out of Beurling. There was plenty to do, and plenty to learn.

Take formation flying. I did Lord knows how many hours of it at OTU, and when I left I could fly wingtip to wingtip with anybody. That's not talking big. Everybody who rides the Spits can—or he can't fly Spitters. Day in and day out, in long stretches, we'd be up there in Vs, or V of Vs, or echelon, or line abreast or astern, moving in and out of respective formations when Larry Philpott, our Canadian instructor, who'd flown with Bader in the Battle of Britain and been shot down, gave us the signal to take up line astern, bring you back to the V, or to take up echelon positions to port or starboard. Those are the signals when there's no radio telephone to talk on. When the RT's plugged in, the leader's orders come through by voice. By the time those hours were up there wasn't a man on the course who couldn't practically take off in formation, make tight turns, dive, climb and do all the tricks of team flying as a piece of the whole.

Oxygen climbs were another of our specialties at

OTU, something else you need to know all about before you start attacking Jerry sweeps at 28,000 feet. In the Spitfire two bottles of oxygen are placed in the fuselage and before taking off you attach a tube on your own equipment to the end of another tube leading from the bottles into the cockpit. The mask covers nose, mouth and chin, and the RT mike is built into it, so you're always wearing the thing and might as well get used to it from the start. A lever on the left-hand side of the cockpit controls the flow and gives the user the height adjustment. In combat flying you begin to feed the oxygen to yourself about the time you hit 10,000 feet and continually adjust the flow as you climb into rarer atmosphere. The effect is to make you feel grandly alive, clearheaded. I did three oxygen climbs at OTU, going to 31,000 feet the first time, 36,000 the second, and on the third climb to better than 38,000.

We spent plenty of time scrambling, too, parking all our equipment, bar Mae Wests, in our aircraft and sitting around a hut near the aircraft, reading or writing or talking among ourselves. Then suddenly Lacey, or whoever happened to be running the show, would snap: "Okay, Beurling, Seed, Allen. Scramble!" The trio called would pour out the door and run for their ships. You'd jump into your parachute as you hit the cockpit, throwing the straps over the shoulders and locking it to the flying suit. Next you fasten the Sutton

"SCRAMBLE"

harness, which holds you in the seat, taking a strap over each shoulder and one over each thigh and locking them in the same spot, in front of the tummy, where the chute clamps in (to bale, you simply pull a pin and the Sutton harness falls off). Then come helmet, goggles and oxygen mask, finally gloves. After that you taxi out, turn into the wind, and get the hell into the air. If all this takes more than two minutes you're no scrambler. If you're smart, you're airborne in a minute and a half.

Scrambles on actual operations, of course, usually take in more planes than we used in practice at OTU. Most of the time you'll get three squadrons—that's 36 Spitfires—working together, each taking its turn as readiness squadron, in daily rotation. Each squadron breaks down into three flights of fours, and of these one is always on immediate call, ready to be off the ground in two minutes or better. The first quartette in any squadron is always "Red Section," the others probably Yellow and Blue. When Red scrambles, the next quartette moves into immediate readiness. If the whole readiness squadron is scrambled, then the second duty squadron moves in, ready to go. Technically they're supposed to have thirty minutes' leeway, but many's the time I've seen 'em all gone in five. That's the general theory of scrambling, but it doesn't always work according to theory when the scrambling is done in a place like Malta, because rules don't go

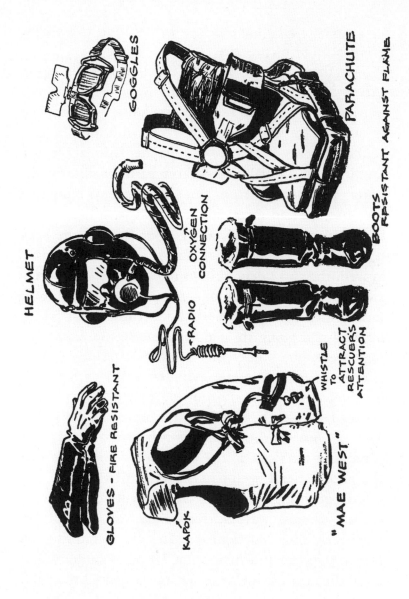

GOGGLES

PARACHUTE

BOOTS
RESISTANT AGAINST FLAME

HELMET

OXYGEN
CONNECTION

RADIO

WHISTLE
TO
ATTRACT
RESCUERS
ATTENTION

GLOVES - FIRE RESISTANT

KAPOK

"MAE WEST"

in a free-for-all. Then it's readiness for everybody, every minute of the day.

In these shows at OTU we flew in full combat gear, sitting around the dispersal hut in our Mae Wests, waiting for the call to race for our Spits, hook up, and get away. The Mae West—the name indicates the part of the anatomy it covers—is a padded life jacket, yellow in color to make its wearer easily visible in the water. It fastens in front with a couple of tapes and four buttons and through the crotch with tapes hanging front and back, to be tied off. Behind the neck is a big kapok-filled collar and the front is kapoked as well, the two fillers being so designed as to prevent an injured or unconscious man's head from going underwater backwards, and to keep him from falling forward and going in face first. Inside the kapok linings are rubber tubes and on the left side in front is fastened a small metal cylinder, filled with carbon dioxide. A lever on the outside of the jacket, when released, breaks the cylinder and blows up the jacket. You can float in the things forever, even if you're injured and can't get at the blowup lever. Mae is sure the pilot's friend, well-named, from all I hear.

Dogfighting, practiced only by subterfuge in the earlier schools, was tackled all-out as part of the combat-training curriculum. In the beginning we fought pupil against instructor. Later, as students mastered the art of surprise attack and acquired the confidence to go in for the kill, pupil and pupil would square off against each other and merry sky battles would ensue. Mostly I worked out with Bill Allen on these parties, and he sure put up stiff opposition. The two of us would split-ass all over the sky, up through the clouds and down again, each trying to get on the other's tail, or between his opponent and the sun, or into any conceivable position for a shot. When you figured you had him you'd snap the camera gun and wave to your opponent that you'd potted him. After that you'd either start all over again or quit and go down, depending on how long you'd been at it and the state of the gas supply. That doesn't mean that every time you *thought* you had a bead on the other fellow you'd snap the camera. Not by a jugful. You weren't going home with a lot of pictures of empty sky if you could help it—and you can help it plenty by waiting until you *know* you've got him. Great fun!

Dogfighting and air-to-air gunnery practice were the two spots where I could really go to work on deflection theories, find out if all the book learning I'd been absorbing for months meant anything in practice. The ground target stuff didn't mean a thing, because you're firing on a rigid target and I never met a Jerry or an Eyetie yet who'd sit still while you put a burst into him. But firing on the drogue—that's RAFese for a towed target—was sport, even though the target flew a steady course and didn't horse around the sky. After all, the pilot of the towing aircraft isn't anxious to get himself shot up with live ammunition, though it's happened before now and the poor guys have had to bale.

An old Fairey-Battle, specially armored, tows the drogue out over the sea at about 2,000 feet, and the pupil's job is to come in on it in his Spitfire from the opposite direction and approximately equal altitude. As he meets the drogue, the Spit pilot turns in on it, as if to swing behind in line astern, but cuts his turn when on an angle of about forty-five degrees and off to either starboard or port, and lets the drogue have a burst, which should finish when the attacker is on an angle of approximately thirty degrees and either climbing or diving away. That ensures that your ammunition won't go running ahead, shooting the tail off the Fairey, two hundred yards or so out in front.

I had good luck with my first air-to-air tests. My first burst blew the drogue clear away from its mother ship, severing the cable. The next time I put so much stuff into the drogue itself that I shot it to pieces. The Deflection theories worked. The midnight oil was paying off.

What was all this theorizing I talk about so much? All pretty simple, really. You know that a cannon shell travels 2,800 feet in a second. You know your enemy is flying at, say, 300 miles an hour and you know what you're doing yourself. Well, deflection shooting, roughly, is the result of relating all these known speeds, from all of which you get a pretty fair idea where your opponent is going to be at a given instant. Then you let go your squirt to be there when he arrives, provided he doesn't change course en route. That all sounds pretty complicated, but when you keep working on it the thing almost becomes second nature. Your instincts tell you what to do.

The long and short of the fighter pilot's business sum up about like this. There are three factors: flying, shooting, and the physical fitness, plus eyesight, of the pilot. Take the last one out, simply by saying it's vital. You need the kind of fitness which makes you so keen you just live to fly. As to flying and gunnery, let me put it this way: You can be the best precision pilot in the world, but if you don't know how to shoot, you won't get Jerries; and you can be the best shot above-ground, but if you can't fly like Billy-be-damned, then Jerry will knock you off. If you skid or slip around the sky, then every burst will go wide of the mark. So it's flying and shooting together that do the trick. Only when the two have merged and become one co-ordinated instinct can you expect to shoot down more than the odd accidentally hit enemy.

(ROBERTS: I'd better take this over for a minute, simply because we're running head-on into a young man who'll "be damned if he's going to talk like God to every pilot in the United Nations."

"Okay, friend," I said, "but you shot down twenty-nine enemy aircraft, mostly by deflection shooting!"

"So I shot down twenty-nine Huns and Eyeties," George answered. "So what? Does that entitle me to tell everybody else what to do?"

"Not what to do, but how to do it," I explained soothingly.

Well, the secret is in that merging of flying and shooting, when the aircraft, the pilot, and the guns become one fighting unit, not three. Too many good pilots—and there aren't any dud Spitfire pilots—think of flying and shooting as separate entities, of shooting as something you do when you've finally worked your way onto the tail of Hun or Eyetie. You've got to work on your flying and your shooting until you've made them one.

Then there's a lot of people who fly and shoot by the book . . . learn what they're taught, fly when they're told to fly, scatter tracer all over the sky. When they discover they've flown right out of the last page of the book and are faced with some problem they never heard of before, they're stuck, because they've never improvised. The long and short of it is that being a fighter pilot is an all-time job. You've got to live for it twenty-four hours a day. And that's what Beurling did. Hence all those Huns, all but three or four of which went down because the attack came from an unexpected quarter. One other point: Don't fire on your enemy until you're sure you've got him, or something precious close to it! Don't tip your hand by spraying lead all over the heavenly firmament! They used to call it not shooting until you could see the whites of their eyes.

"Right," I said. "Now what about personal habits? What about this exemplary life of yours we hear so much about? Where do we go from there?"

George thought that one over for a minute.

"Listen," he said, "you can't shoot Jerry down with a hangover, any more than you can with mirrors. But that's got nothing to do with a man's personal habits, so long as he's moderate. I don't take a drink and I don't smoke; never did. That's because I neither want nor need liquor or tobacco. Right. That's just the way I am. But there's plenty of fellows who need the letdown they can get from a good, stiff drink. Some guys would never get their nervous systems untangled otherwise—when the job's done for the day, I mean. I didn't shoot down a lot of Huns because I've never had a drink in my life or never smoked a cigarette. I shot 'em down because I took my flying seriously, lived for it, learned the score about deflection shooting and kept my eyes peeled—all but a couple of times!"

"That clears that up," I said.)

The minute you slide into the cockpit of a Spitfire for the first time you realize you've acquired an office in which you're going to be an extremely busy fellow. Exactly what nonflying people think a fighter pilot's job consists of, I don't know, but from what I've picked up in ordinary conversation I sort of get the idea the general opinion is that you simply slide into a comfortable, if slightly cramped, seat, switch on the engine, and fly away. After that you throw the thing around the sky until you get your sights on a German. Then you shoot the German and come home. Maybe people don't make it quite so simple as that in their minds, but that would seem to be the approach. If that was the case, pretty nearly everybody would be flying Spitfires.

Probably in no space in the world of equal size is so much scientific equipment packed, all of it built around an aperture just large enough to accommodate one adult. His seat, comfortable enough, but not roomy, armored from the seat of his pants to the top of his head, must also accommodate the harness which fastens him to the aircraft, plus the parachute, complete with rubber dinghy, which .offers him an alternate way home under certain unpleasant circumstances. Behind him, in the fuselage, are his oxygen supply and the compressed air which operates guns and brakes. Ahead of the pilot, eye-high, are the almost innumerable gadgets which let him know how he's getting along from moment to moment—the air speed indicator and the gyro compass, his artificial horizon, the altimeter, gauges to tell him the bad news about his fuel supply, the pressure and temperature of his oil, the state of the glycol in his cooling system. Others inform him about his generator and the number of revolutions of the airscrew. There's a switch to turn on his navigation lights and the usual run-of-mill compass. At one side he has a couple of buttons with which to fumble when the big battery for his engine starter is wheeled out on a trolley and plugged in under one wing. Off in a corner of the panel is his air pressure gauge. At eye level is his gunsight. So much for what's before his eyes.

Hitched to the side of the fuselage, within easy

reach of a hand, is a box arrangement containing a lever to control his throttle mixture and another for regulating the pitch of his propeller. Over on the other side of the fuselage is the lever to lift up and let down his undercart. On the right hand-side of the cockpit is still another control, this one for the shutters of his radiator, which sits under the right wing, to keep the glycol in the cooling system at proper temperature. Left and forward, on the panel, is the lever for raising and lowering the landing flaps.

The young man, then, has these odds and ends to watch and think about while he takes off, flies, and returns to earth. In addition he must fly, sight his guns, shoot, keep his eyes peeled for Jerries, and watch his own position in formation or for other aircraft in his path in a general melee. He could use a couple more pairs of hands, but there's no room for them, and a pair of eyes in the back of his head would come in more than handy.

When you graduate to Spitfires you acquire a compact instrument of sudden death, for the enemy if you can get him in range, for yourself if you don't keep your wits about you. Into thirty-six feet of space, wingtip to wingtip, are packed two cannon and four machine guns, usually harmonized to bring their most devastating fire to bear on a point three hundred yards ahead, plus shells for the cannon in tension drums and ammunition for the Browning machine guns, in

either belts or pans. Mostly your machine-gun ammunition will alternate—incendiary, tracer, ball, and
armor piercing; that for the cannon the same, without
tracer. Guns are fired by three buttons on the control
column. Number One lets go the machine guns alone,
Number Three the cannon alone, Number Two gives
out with all you've got.

There are other implements and gadgets, of course.
There's the radio telephone to plug in, the oxygen to
hook up, the sights to adjust on a ground target before
taking off. In short, the Spitfire, with its wings full of
gas and ammunition and better than a thousand horses
compressed into its Merlin engine, is equipped with
practically everything you can think of, except room
service.

From all this, however, don't infer that the pilot is
simply a poor bloke sitting in the middle of potential
inferno, to whose well-being the designer has given no
thought. The way our people see him, he is a highly
expensive piece of equipment, trained for a year before being sent into battle, and therefore, apart from
the humanities, a piece of bric-a-brac to be tended
with as much care as the circumstances permit. His
seat is well-armored, his ship, of all-metal construction,
tough as nails. You can bring her down on her belly,
hanging on the prop until she slakens down to about
seventy miles an hour, drag the tail and let her flop,
and if you've been lucky enough to pick soft ground

she won't slide more than twenty yards. The pilot's body and feet are far enough behind the engine that he doesn't get the real bump. The one place you avoid like the plague in a belly landing is asphalt, or any similar substance, because you don't want to go stirring up any sparks to ignite gas or the glycol in the cooling system. Actually a Spit is infinitely less a firetrap than most single-seaters, however. You can't jettison your gas, and leaking glycol is always a fire hazard, but if you've cut your switches and picked soft ground, the chances of taking fire in a crash landing are reasonably low.

So that's what we'd come down to OTU to learn about. And learn we did. Spits were all over the sky, in all kinds of weather, in formation, dogfighting, split-assing, doing all the things which, added together, comprise combat flying. All that was missing from the scene to make it complete, was the enemy. He'd be the next stop, the stop at the end of the line!

We went to work without fuss or frills, about fifty of us to a class and a number of classes passing through the unit in various stages of training. We flew and we flew and we flew, and when we didn't fly we'd be perched in the Link trainer, practicing every mortal thing that can happen to airborne man, so that in emergency a pilot will do the right thing by second nature. Not until he comes to that point can you call him a pilot.

Under such conditions we had our share of crack-ups, fatal and otherwise, tragic and comic. Of my own flight, totaling fifteen pupils, two were killed at OTU, Pronk, an Australian, and Moreau, a lad from South America. They were practicing head-on attacks over the coast, pulled out too late and collided. Moreau's ship simply blew to pieces, and he hadn't a chance to bale out. Pronk hit a hillside before he could get his aircraft under control and himself out of the cockpit.

None of the other smackups in our flight were fatal, two or three were comic as hell. Like the day Bob and Paul went low-flying . . .

Down near the coast Bob got the brilliant idea it would be fun to dive on a flock of gulls and give the birds a scare. He went into a steep dive and as Bob went down the gulls went up. Bob must have hit about twenty of them as he tried to duck. They smashed the hood over his cockpit. They put dents in his wings. A couple jammed his gunports. Blood and feathers were spattered all over the aircraft. Even a gull's leg stuck to one of his wings. Meanwhile Paul was busy trying to get through the cloud of rising birds and flew down so low that he hit the water with his prop and bent it all to the devil. Two badly frightened young pilots limped home to OTU and landed. No more gull-scaring for them!

I know I want no part of gulls. I hit one by accident one day, while low-flying. The damned bird put a

dent the size of a football into the leading edge of my
port wing, and the shudder that went through the
Spit when I hit it was like bouncing off a wall.

The funniest mixup of all, however, happened to
one of our three Hollanders, van der Stok, later killed
with 41 Squadron, just before I joined them. Van was
beetling along at about 5,000 feet when suddenly his
engine cut out. He looked around and picked out a
nice, cozy field and went on down. As he came in he
spotted a big pile of straw and decided to land
just short of it, to assure himself of something nice
and soft to stop his run. So far, so good. Unfortunately, however, Van's undercarriage struck a rock
and ground-looped him, rump-over-teakettle, into the
straw pile. Straw pile, my eye! The straw was the usual
covering for the farmer's manure heap, and the poor
old Dutchman was catapulted into it head first. Believe me, Van didn't get into mess for a couple of days.
That Essence de Vache was passionate stuff!

Seems to me the all-time high in comedy crashes
was one which happened to a guy named Tilley, however. Tilley and myself and another chap were out on
formation flying, I as leader, when we were caught
in a sudden snowstorm quite a distance from home.
Halfway back Tilley broke off and decided to look
for a drome on his own. The other lad and I got back
all right, but no sign of Tilley until next morning,
when he limped in from a little town twenty miles

away, after cadging rides and making his way back as best he could, minus one Spitfire. He explained that he had been unable to spot a landing field, so had flown south to try to get away from the snow. The snow was everywhere, however, so he'd turned north again and finally picked up a largish field that looked empty. He came in and tried to land, but couldn't see a thing, particularly a tree, which he hit with a wing. That gave him a bit of a scare, so he gunned and took off, flying through a flock of telephone wires on his way out. He got away with that and kept flying. Through the muck he spotted a small emergency field and tried to slip into it. Overshooting, he gunned, tripped on the far fence, pulled up and went around again. This time he undershot—the poor guy couldn't see a thing through the solid bank of soft snow blobs —scraped the near fence, pranged against another tree and, so help me, got away with it and into the air again. Tilley was still going strong and developing a growing faith in his ability to fly himself out of trouble. But the engine was getting a bit sick of the business and, in protest, started shooting back flame. So Tilly yanked back the stick and went up to about 800 feet, where he swished over onto his back and baled, head first. "First time in my life I ever saw snow going up!" he said, as he recounted his experiences to a gang roaring with merriment when he got home in the morning. Nobody would believe his tall tale, of course. But later in the day we all flew over to take a look. The guy was right. Wires were down, trees were barked, fences knocked over, exactly as he'd described. Don't ever tell me a Spitfire can't take it!

Tilley—a good pilot, no matter the yarn—was fined one pound for that escapade for "a major crash, causing the write-off of a machine, due to Pilot Error." The quid went into the common fund, the purpose of which was to set aside a sum of money, raised through individual misfortunes, for a big class blow-out at the end of the course. Landing with a dead prop cost you a shilling, bending a prop or other slight damage cost five shillings, a down-wind landing seven-and-six. If you were careless and took off with your airscrew at coarse pitch, that would be ten shillings, please. Landing without undercarriage, or any major crackup arising from the pilot's own carelessness, cost the even pound. Adjudicator of fines was Ginger Lacey, our flight commander, and Tilley was assessed for breaking away from formation and losing a ship. By the end of the course Lacey held almost £40 in trust for the gang and everybody went to town. What a night that was! I guess Tilley didn't begrudge his donation. The harps had been twanging right in his ears for a few minutes.

Plenty of chaps dusted themselves off and walked away from crashes which might easily have proved

fatal. Sergeant Fletcher, an Englishman, was one example. His engine cut out as he was circling over the
drome, and he stretched his glide too fine to try to
get in over the wires. The Spitter stalled and dived-in
the last thirty feet. Fletcher walked away unhurt. Yet
the same thing, happening to another guy, might
finish him completely. It all depends on what you hit,
and what hits you.

There was an Aussie lad, for instance, who hit a
near-by river while flying along at about 250 miles
an hour. His angle was such that he knifed right
through the water and, so help me, bub, took fire as
he hit. The old Spitter, burning, actually flew underwater, while the Australian calmly pried up the hood
and swam away. I personally saw a Czech pupil crash
into the mud flats beside the same river and smash his
Spitter to bits. Another good guy gone, I thought, as
I flew back to the drome to report the crash. Imagine
my surprise when they told me at the orderly room
that the pilot had just phoned for transportation
home. He hadn't even bruised himself!

Such things were considered comic, but there was
tragedy aplenty, though not much was ever said about
that. One of the most popular lads on the course, an
Englishman, was quietly slipping into the field with
a Spitter one day and didn't even see a Master, coming
in to land immediately beneath him. The Master's
pilot was completely in the wrong, for he had been

making a long, flat approach, when he should have come in short and curving, touching his wheels down just as he leveled out from his final turn. That knowledge didn't help the Spitter pilot's personal feelings a bit, however, when his metal prop sheared the tail off the Master, which dived-in and burst into flame. The pilot was dragged out, badly burned, and rushed to hospital, where the sawbones amputated both his legs and one arm. The poor guy died in the night.

Then there was another English chap, Sergeant Cox, who simply disappeared and never came back from a cross-country flight alone. He was found three weeks later, his aircraft almost undamaged, perched on the top of Mount Snowdon, with poor old Coxie dead in the cockpit, because two broken legs had made it impossible for him to get out of the ship.

So it went along. For days on end everything would coast along swimmingly. Then tragedy would strike again. A Fighting French lad would stall, spin in, and kill himself . . . A Ferry bloke, bringing a new Spitter to the OTU, would bump into a hill, flying blind in an unexpected storm . . . A couple of chaps would be seriously practicing formation flying, acting as targets for another lad who'd been sent up to polish up his diving. He'd dive too close and hit both aircraft, as he tried to go through between . . . One pilot would bale, the other'd spin in and be killed. Such things are all part of the game. You can't

make fighter pilots out of human raw material until
you let 'em go to town and fly. But every now and
then somebody is bound to make a mistake. Then
tragedy happens. I know Bill Allen and I damn nearly
killed each other by the simplest little quirk you could
imagine, each blacking out momentarily in sudden
turns while practicing head-on attacks. Each revived
in the nick! Thank God, Bill pulled up and I dived!
Otherwise it would have been curtains for a couple
more would-be combat pilots.

The all-time high in flying tragedies for the station
came at the beginning of December, however. They
still call that day Black Friday around the OTU, I'm
told. That day we lost seven aircraft and twelve aircrew people, thanks to the unpredictable English
weather. It all sounds so damned simple when you
try to describe what happened.

A snowstorm blew in from the sea about two
o'clock in the afternoon, while the day's work was in
full swing. Because the station lies in "weather-
making" country, probably the people in the control
tower and the meteorological boys thought it just-
another-of-those-things. So, by the time they tried to
get everybody down it was too late. The snow raced
in from the sea and sat on the country like a blanket,
in huge soft blobs which rubbed everything out. I
know what it was like, because I was one of the mugs
trying to find home and from fifty feet you could just

see the treetops, but not a sign of the ground. Fortunately, my course had worked out all right and I picked up the black line of the asphalt runway on the field as I came over it at thirty feet. Two of us were together, and we went around again, wingtip to wingtip, talking to each other on our mikes. As soon as we crossed the hangars we lost sight of the field and ground again. We swung around wide, while we made up our minds what to do, agreeing that the other fellow would fall in astern, lower his wheels as I led him in, and land, and that I'd make another circuit before coming in. That's what we did, and we both made it. Most people weren't so lucky! This is Black Friday's grim record:

Pilot Officer Morrison, of the Delivery Flight, was heading for home in a Rapide (the DH-89) with four or five Ferry pilots. In the storm his Venturi tube, which provides all the fluid for the instrument panel, iced up, with the result that the only way he could tell how he was riding in the muck, diving or stalling, or level, was by the engine sounds. He ordered all his passengers to bale, and all reached the ground safely, while Morrison and the copilot stayed behind, trying to keep going until they could see something. They stalled at 2,000 feet and dived-in over open country not far from the drome. One aircraft. Two men gone.

Next on the list was a New Zealand lad, a pilot officer, who lost his way in the mess and simply hit the deck, just outside a near-by town. Two planes, three pilots.

An English lad, a pupil in my class, apparently tried to get up over the muck, the top of which was away up at 18,000. At 5,000 something happened and he lost control, spun in and crashed. Three aircraft, four men gone.

A Wellington had taken off just before the storm came up and, trying to get back, hit a house about three-quarters of a mile from the drome. The house was badly damaged, but its inmates escaped unhurt. Not so the three fellows in the Wellington. All were killed. That made the toll four aircraft and seven men.

Another lad, flying a Hurricane away, heading south, crashed into a mountainside. Five ships. Eight men.

Another DH-89 completed the list of fatal accidents. Manned by a pilot and three air-gunners, it was en route to the OTU from the Midlands, when it crashed about twelve miles short of home. All were killed. That made the grisly total of six aircraft destroyed and twelve men killed—a record seldom tied during the blitzes on Malta. The seventh ship was a Spit, flown by a pupil, who escaped unhurt from a write-off crash. An hour later the storm had passed over and the sun was shining again. Not one of the better days!

Before Black Friday was out of our systems the

course finished and kids of a dozen nationalities who had horsed all over the skies of northwestern England together for almost three months said our good-byes and wished each other good hunting in the days ahead. Bob, Paul, Bill, and I all went separate ways. Bill I haven't seen since. The last I heard he was still going strong, out in the Middle East, knocking 'em off for Montgomery and the Eighth Army. Bob and Paul and I have bumped into each other in tougher places, of which more later.

It had been a grand three months, during which I'd learned more about the job ahead than in the three years which preceded the final-training stages. Grand instructors. Swell people for classmates. Everybody keen as mustard. Good living. Good grub. The ᷆eeling that you were on your way at last. It was the first station I'd ever left with any regrets. To cap everything came Ginger Lacey's offer to recommend me for commissioned rank. I said: "No, sir. I better stay the way I am. I feel like a pilot, but not like an officer." "Have it your own way," he said and off I went to pack my kit. I was a fighting pilot at last. Or was I?

CHAPTER IV

Over Hitler's Europe

IF there ever was a guy right up on the bit, that guy was me, sitting in the corner of a second-class railway carriage out of London's Liverpool Street station on December 16, 1941, watching the flatlands of Essex go by. There I was, on my way to join 403 Squadron and become a member of the most famous Spitfire outfit in Britain, 11 Group. To have learned in London that I was joining a mob whose pilots were almost all Canadians, graduates of my own country's huge Air Training Plan, was an extra reason for rejoicing, even though the RCAF had turned me down back home. I'd be flying with fellows who talked my kind of language. That's no slam aimed at any other breed. I'd been flying for months with swell guys from all over the world. But, hell! I'm a Canuck. Why wouldn't I want to go into my first action with my own countrymen? Who wouldn't?

What would the job be like? Would we be flying sweeps over Occupied France every day? How would

I stand up under enemy fire? How would my own shooting work out when Huns were shooting at me? All the questions which must pour through every freshman's mind as he's on his way to join his first service squadron raced through mine as the train rattled through the marshy country which lies behind the East Coast. London seemed barely left behind before we were sliding into the station where I'd been told to pile out.

What does a guy do next? I wondered, piling my kit and looking around. Does somebody meet you? Do they send the town car, or the limousine? Right then a good, solid Canadian voice said in my ear: "Looking for 403 Squadron? Like to share a taxi?"

We introduced ourselves to each other. He was Sergeant Collison, out of Hamilton, Ontario, on his way back from leave. Okay, fella, let's grab a cab and get rolling.

I pelted Collison with questions throughout the six-mile drive to the drome. What was the squadron doing, most of the time? Well, things were pretty quiet, lots of convoy patrols, but not many sweeps lately. Did Jerry bother you much on these shows? Hell, no. You'd go for days and days without seeing a sign of him. How about raids over here? Pretty quiet. Pretty quiet. Every now and then a Ju 88 might sneak over, hit and run. But it looked like the dull season was setting in. This damned English weather. You're acquainted with the English weather, old man? I said, yes, I'd met it. Sell you my share of it for a plugged nickel, or call it a cup of Childs' coffee. Hell, said Collison, I haven't had a Christian cup of coffee since I left Hamilton, and that was way back when Judas Iscariot was a rookie aircraftman.

At the orderly room the adjutant took me and my logbook in to the CO, Squadron Leader Pinky Douglas, a Scot and one of the two non-Canadians in 403, who looked me and the record over and remarked, sort of sternly: "You've got some good assessments here, sergeant, but because you've done well at school doesn't mean you'll do well in a squadron. Here you've got to obey orders and fly as you're told." From there he went on to intimate that, in his opinion, Canadians are likely to be wild, undisciplined fellows and that not all the superflying in Christendom can ever make up for these liabilities. Wing Commander Paddy Finucane, D.S.O. and Bar, plus a triple D.F.C., had never been a particularly outstanding flier, the CO said, but he had qualities of leadership and steadiness far more important than superb flying skill. So had Wing Commander Tuck, with a D.S.O. and triple D.F.C. for his 27 Heinies against Finucane's 32. Tuck at that time, like the magnificent Paddy, was flying in 11 Group. Now both are gone: Finucane into the Channel; Tuck to eke out the rest of the war in a German prison camp.

Collison was waiting outside the orderly room when I made my long-faced exit. "Cut you down to size?" he grinned.

"And how," I said.

"I well remember," he said. " 'You've got some good assessments here, sergeant, but . . .' That's part of the initiation, the baptism of fire. But Pinky's okay. Heart of gold under the stern exterior. Grab your kit and I'll show you where you live."

The sergeant pilots were bedded down in an evacuated house near the field, three or four to a room, and the mess was in amongst the buildings alongside the drome itself. I moved into one of the smaller bedrooms, occupied by Art Monserez, a Westerner, in solitary style until I came along. That night Art took me round and made me acquainted with the guys who would be my buddies in B Flight all through the winter: Larry Somers of Simcoe, Ontario, Bill Munn, Schmitz, Crawford, Pilot Officer Norm Dick from Kenora, and Flying Officer Gillespie, the flight commander. Collison and Monserez rounded out the gang. The commander of A Flight was Flight Lieutenant Timber Wood, a grand Englishman. Mac Macdonald, a nephew of Roy Brow, the Canadian who shot Richthofen down in the last war and just as good a pilot as his uncle ever was, was in 403 when first I knew the outfit. Crist and Ryckman, both future Malta scramblers, French-Canadian Johnny Rainville,

Belcher, a prairie farmer, Hubbard, and Magwood were other members of the squadron that winter. They were a damned good gang, as I'd find out to my sorrow when I parted company with them.

Almost before I'd moved in and settled down we all packed up and moved across country to the other side of London, leaving our field to 71 Squadron, one of the old Eagle bunch. Actually we sat around for the better part of four days, waiting for the pea soup to lift and let us fly over to our new home. Before the muck came down I'd flown a brief sector reconnaissance to get to know the surrounding country and an hour's formation with Collison, just to check my flying. We moved out of the old homestead on the 24th, sharing our new drome with another of the Eagle squadrons and with 222, commonly known as Treble-2, a highly international RAF mob mustering Englishmen, Americans, Canadians, Fighting Frenchmen, Dutchmen, Czechs, and Poles on its pilot roster, among them my old pal Bob Seed, who promptly grabbed me as if we hadn't laid eyes on each other for a year and said: "Sweetheart, put on your hat. You and I are going up to town for dinner!"

Christmas Day, 1941, was a damned sight happier than the one I'd put in the year before down in Devon. Cripes! Had I been in this show for two Christmases and not heard a shot fired for keeps yet? But never mind that . . . This was a *good* Christmas,

which is more than you could have said about the
other one. The sergeants celebrated the day by serving
dinner for the erks, the lads who look after the ships
and keep guys like us flying and coming back. The
show was a lot of fun, with plenty of ribbing sailing
both ways. Great guys, most erks. My kind, anyway.
You can really sit around and fan with them. They
like to talk engines and guns and instruments and
suchlike, each according to his own trade. Any pilot
can learn a lot from the boys who look after his ship,
and at the same time make friends who'll go through
hell and high water for him. If he's an any-good person, a pilot picks up six foster fathers in the blokes
who look after him and his Spitter.

Before Christmas dinner I flew what I suppose
would be counted my first combat flight, a convoy
patrol with three other aircraft between Clacton-on-
Sea and the mouth of the Thames. For action it was
about as exciting as Sunday in Toronto, just beetling
up and down over a bunch of ships hugging the English coast and nothing happening. That night Bob and
I raided the kitchen over at Treble-2's officers' mess,
collecting the better part of a turkey, complete with
cranberry sauce and gravy, plus a Christmas pudding,
with which we stuffed ourselves in Bob's room until
we were both ready for the stomach pump. When you
run into solid North American grub in England the
idea is to eat all you can hold while you can get it.

Tomorrow it'll be Brussels sprouts again. Of that you can always be certain.

That winter sure was a honey for a bunch of guys supposed to be in a war up to their ailerons. Bar a flock of convoy patrols and three or four routine scrambles to meet raiders which never came, not a thing happened to us for close to three months. It wasn't just us. The whole London area and the country clear down to the coasts was literally stiff with Spitfires sitting on their sterns waiting for Jerry to come over and start something. But he couldn't get at us, nor we at him. Our Number One Enemy all through January and February was the climate. God! How it could rain! And for fine days we had fog.

During January, 1942, we swapped COs, acquiring Squadron Leader Campbell, D.F.C., as our new boss. To judge him by his first remarks to his pilots on arrival he wasn't exactly full-out for Canadians, a viewpoint which, he told us, "it's up to you chaps to change." The gang did that little thing okay, when the time came to go into action for him. Canucks may not spend as much time as they should springing to attention, and maybe we don't draw as sharp a line as we might between officer pilots and sergeant pilots. But, if I can be forgiven one race-proud crack, we can hold our own once we're off the floor. Just a difference in national customs that gives us a different outlook, I guess. You can't put three thousand miles of ocean between a couple of nations, most of the citizens of which see each other only when they get together to lick the Huns and expect them to be alike in ways and ideas, even though they do belong to the same empire.

Funny thing about the new SL. He sure stepped off on the wrong foot with the boys. But over the long pull he turned out to be a good egg. That's the way it usually goes. There aren't many drips in this business.

We lost only two pilots during the winter doldrums: Art Monserez, my first roomie, and a fellow named Cawsey, who arrived late in January. Both were accidents.

Monserez went out to do a bit of practice flying one January day and, coming in to land, couldn't get his undercart to lock down. Art went up again, apparently to see if a steep dive wouldn't give him a little help, but got into a spin coming down through the clouds. He checked the first spin, but promptly went into another, the other way, and spun right in.

Cawsey's death happened during a scramble to meet a lone Hun raider, but it wasn't the Jerry who got him. He and Mac Macdonald took off to do the job and chased the German into a cloud at 12,000 feet. Instead of pulling over alongside Mac as they went into the wool, Cawsey followed him line astern and sliced off Mac's tail with his prop. Cawsey was never seen again, and the assumption was that he must have gone into the sea.

Mac himself had the hell of a time baling out, but somehow got the Spit over on her back and broke away. He drifted down into the Channel and was picked up by the rescue launch after floating around in his rubber dinghy for twenty minutes.

These RAF dinghies are really Something for the poor bloke who has to take to the silk over water, as I know only too well. The dinghy comes as part of the parachute pack, and actually is the insides of the cushion under your rump. Just before you hit the water, if you're wise and have a good memory, you release the big umbrella, but the dinghy stays with you, dangling by a ring from your Mae West. As you float with Mae you rip the cover off the dinghy, pull a pin which releases the tap on the bottle of CO_2 inside, and the dinghy slowly inflates and becomes a rubber boat five feet long. Then all you have to do is grab a couple of loops on the side and pull yourself aboard, all set to take up light housekeeping. The designers haven't missed a trick.

Stowed aboard you'll find bandages, rum, concentrated food tablets, chocolate, a couple of paddles which fit over the hands on loops, rubber plugs for emergency repairs, a rubber bucket for baling, another collapsible bucket to use as a sea anchor, plus a yellow cap to pull over your head and make you easy for the boys in the rescue launch to find. The dinghy itself is designed for comfort and you can loll back in a corner and take it easy until the wrecking crew turns up—and over in the English Channel country the launch lads will often run close into the coast of Occupied France to fetch a pilot home.

Meanwhile, as we moved along toward spring and the expectation of action, several new pilots arrived to strengthen the roster of 403. One was Pilot Officer Zoochkan. Zooch, who later went down into the Channel, was sure no red-tape officer. Everybody knew him for a swell egg. About the same time Flight Lieutenant Brad Walker came over from one of the Hurri-bomber outfits as a flight commander. Teddy Argue, Hurst, Aitken, and Claire Walker were other newcomers, all Canucks. That was the shape of things on March 8th, when we went out on our first sweep of the spring, escorting half a dozen Bostons while they laid eggs on some kind of a war plant at Comines, near Lille.

We lost Aitken that day, on his first show. He got picked off the tail end of the formation by a Messerschmitt 109F. The rest of the show was okay. 403's job was close escort—right alongside the bombers, that is—and although we could see plenty of Jerries, our assignment was to stay right with those Bostons and pay no attention to Huns, unless they got down through the top screen. Not one came down on my side. Timber Wood picked off an Me which butted in on his side—just a couple of tight circles, a quick burst, and down went the Schmitt. That made Timber's fourth German Destroyed, plus a couple of Probables, and he collected a D.F.C. a few days later. Hurst's Spit was pretty well shot up in a tangle he got into with a couple of other Me's which broke through the cover escort. A cannon shell went through his port aileron. On the way back he landed on an airdrome near the coast to look the damage over. His ship was still airworthy, so he refueled and flew home. That was my first taste of real action. It was swell fun, though none of the mixings came my way.

Those sweeps over France that spring were really fancy shows. Sometimes as many as 200 Spitfires would step out to shield half a dozen bombers. Up on the ceiling two whole wings would fly. They were the guys charged with keeping the Huns away from the big jobs and, therefore, the lads who got most of the dogfighting. Then a couple of thousand feet above the bombers another two wings of fighters would fly. There'd be another wing at close escort; that's right with the big crates. Immediately underneath would be two more wings of Spitters, one to each side. A pretty impressive array we'd be as we made our rendezvous over the coast and set sail for the shores of France.

I was as interested as a kid with a new scooter in the arrangements laid out for that first sweep. On the night of the 7th word came round to the quarters

that we'd be sweeping in the morning and for everybody to get a good night's sleep. Then about 7 A.M.
we all piled into trucks and were driven down to the
dispersal hut of a neighbor squadron, where the whole
wing was briefed by its CO Wing Commander Scott
Malden, D.F.C. (He now wears the D.S.O. as well, plus
a Bar to his D.F.C.) A huge map covered the whole
length of one wall. On it the target was pointed out
and its nature described. Our wing would fly close
escort at 17,000 feet. Other wings would do such-and-
such and thus-and-so. We would form up at a stipu-
lated point over the coast, each outfit at its allotted
height, including the bombers.

Next Malden told us for what purpose each radio
channel would be used, tabbing each with its dis-
tinguishing button on the RT control, one of which
would be for *May Day*—the SOS call of the RAF.
Malden himself would be leading the wing.

"If any of you have trouble," the wingco concluded, "with your engines, radio, or anything else,
turn back. Don't endanger the lives of others by sticking along when you're half crippled. Keep your eyes
peeled, lads. That's all."

We piled into the lorries again and bumped back
to our squadrons. Without delay every man tumbled
into his Spitter and off we went. As soon as we reached
our allotted height we made for the rendezvous, where
the air was full of milling Spitfires, forming-up over

and around the bombers. At 7:35 everybody was in place and off we went, crossing the French coast near Dunkirk about ten minutes later. As we came over France I sat there, taking my first look at the spot where the new Contemptibles had made such a name for themselves not two years before, when it looked as if the show might be lost. I was just getting around to thinking about the other heroes—the guys who went to bring them home—and what a livid hell the place must have been, when *Whambo!!!* A solid flowerbed of flak burst immediately under us and the whole sky went momentarily mad. The reverie was never finished. From then on the job was to fly, keep your eyes peeled, and look out for those six Bostons. I was flying the tail position in Blue Section, right beside the bombers, with Norm Dick immediately in front at Number Three and a newcomer, Don Campbell, from Nova Scotia, alongside at Red Four. We kept plugging along, everybody minding his own business, keeping radio silence until there was something to talk about, and weaving as we flew, just so we wouldn't be sitting-bird targets for any Jerry who might dive through.

Not much flak over Comines that morning, but just as we were turning for home, after the Bostons made their run and laid their eggs smack on the target, about twenty-five Me's from the big field at Abbeville, I guess, turned up and started to play hell. Our gang simply stuck with the bombers. That was our assigned task, and you don't go fooling around with assignments. The mix didn't last long. But Aitken got it, and Wing Commander Eyre, D.F.C., who was being prepped to take over Malden's command, was knocked down too. It was his first sweep over France, though he had bagged seven Huns during the Battle of Britain. He crash-landed in France and was taken prisoner.

All through the dogfight the air was alive with calls on the RT: "Look out, Yellow Four! Messerschmitt coming out of sun at six o'clock. Break left!" A steady flow of dogfight lingo. *Six o'clock* is the position right behind your tail. With a message such as that suddenly breaking through all that Squadron's Yellow foursome would whip around to attack whatever might be coming in on their teammate.

The Germans picked off four Spitters, out of almost two hundred, two from our wing. We scored an even number of Me's and successfully bombed the Comines target. That made it a good show and when we landed an hour and fifty-five minutes after the take-off we were told to wash out for the day. That meant an immediate scurrying for transportation up to London for a lot of high-strung guys!

From the 8th to the 23rd the weather was foul and, although we got in some practice flying around home, no further visits to France were made. We did the odd convoy patrol and whenever the weather was halfway decent I'd grab a Maggie or a Tiger Moth and take the erks sky-riding, one by one. Those ground-bound boys were always grateful for a trip upstairs.

During the March lull my flight commander, Gillespie, asked me if I'd ever thought of going for a commission and offered to recommend me, if I'd like it. I thought it over for a day, but again said no. All my close pals in 403 were sergeants and I'd rather stay living with them, thanks.

"Anyway, sir," I said, "I don't look like officer material to me. Why, it's scarcely any time since they wouldn't even let me in the ranks because I didn't have enough education to suit them. I doubt if I have what they'd consider officer background over here."

"That's fine by me, toots," the flight commander said, "but don't take yourself too damned seriously. Hell, when I was up for my commission the blighters asked me about my background and I grinned right in their ruddy faces. 'My old man is a common laborer,' I told 'em, 'and I'm damned proud of it!' You should have seen their faces!"

(ROBERTS: "Let's take time out," I said, "and dispose of this great moral issue and be done with it. Weren't you being a little bit snooty about your humble estate? How did you get such a bang out of this determination to stay in the ranks?"

Beurling said I had it all wrong. Up to now he hadn't done one solitary thing to rate him for higher status—hadn't so much as put a bullet hole into a German plane, had participated in exactly one sweep over enemy-held territory. Anyway, if I understand him correctly, he doesn't believe in social distinctions. Commissions should be dished out solely on the basis of a man's qualifications to lead, nothing else. He might put it this way: "I would have all pilots rank equally on the ground, the way they rate in the air. I don't go for two sets of social standards on the same job, because I don't think it's good for esprit de corps. That's all."

"Whoa!" I interjected. "The way I understand the thing, the fellows who get commissions with their wings are supposed to be the good students. You were a good student at OTU and Lacey offered to recommend you. At your previous school you were inclined to be an obstreperous kid, so they left you in the ranks. Does that make sense, or doesn't it? Finally you did a real job on Malta and they didn't even ask you—just said, 'Brother, you're a pilot officer!' Doesn't that sound solid to you?"

"Aw, hell!" he concluded. "Maybe I still had a chip on my shoulder. Maybe I was still thinking it was Beurling versus the world! Let's skip it, huh? It isn't that important.")

On the 23rd we did our first fighter sweep of the spring season, going inland as far as Saint-Omer. Nothing happened, though I got my first peek at the Focke-Wulf 190. Plenty of 'em around, but they wouldn't come down and play. On the following day, however, I got all the action I wanted for a couple of minutes, damned nearly too much action!

It was another trip on the Comines run, shaping up pretty much like the previous show, only we were the boys flying top cover this time. Everything was all serene until we were leaving the target, when a flock of Focke-Wulfs came down on us from above. Three of 'em jumped my tail position, their favorite trick (and ours!), to cut me out from the herd and the bastards seemed to be coming at me from every corner of kingdom come. Tracers were putting on a regular fireworks display around the cockpit. I was whipping around in turn after turn, trying my damnedest to get out of harm's way. One guy shot my hood off, just as I was going into a climbing flick roll. The going was getting extremely tough. Looked like almost anything might happen to Mrs. Beurling's boy Georgie, almost any second. I decided to get the hell out of there, *if I could.* Suddenly, as the three Jerries all came at me at once from behind for the kill, I lowered my landing flaps and slowed the old Spitter down to a walk. The Huns all overshot me. By the time they'd turned to come back my flaps were rolled up again and I had pushed on the emergency boot, which gives you extra power for a short time. Young Beurling was heading for home, high-tailing!

Larry Somers got his first Jerry that day, right beside me over Comines. He literally blew the bottom out of that F-W and it went down flaming. All our Spitters came home, but the accompanying wing lost a couple.

Gillespie, who had been transferred to another squadron as a flight commander, was shot down on April 4th, while their outfit and ours were escorting bombers to plaster the shipping at Boulogne. There was sure one good guy!

A series of hapless sweeps followed, up and down the French coast. Plenty of Jerries about. But damned if they wanted any part of us! Then leave came through and off I went to London. For all the good it did me I might as well have stayed on the drome, because I seemed to spend most of the time trying to find a square meal. By that time the sausages were admittedly 85 per cent bread crumbs and actually about 105 per cent. You couldn't buy a hamburger from the Mansion House to Putney. As for hot dogs, my favorite fruit, they haven't even heard of them over there, which is a hell of a way to treat visitors from across the Atlantic. You could get all the tea you could drink, but my tipple is coffee and they still have to make their first potable pot of mocha over in Blighty. Any I swallowed was plain liquid muck. Boy! How I longed for the Great North American Pie Belt, for a juicy steak, for a sackful of hot dogs. Instead I got Brussels sprouts, potatoes and margarine. I went back to the station two days ahead of schedule, primarily because I was hungry.

Back there the news was bad, in more ways than one. Timber Wood had copped it while I was away, a damned popular guy with the whole outfit, an Englishman who made a big hit with his Canadian teammates. I got bad news of another sort when the

orderly room sent for me to tell me I was being transferred. Henceforth 403's personnel would be completely Royal Canadian Air Force and, since I was the
property of the RAF, I'd have to be shuffled along. So
the squadron leader handed me my walking papers,
told me he was sorry to lose me—and away I went to
join a squadron on a drome south and east of the Big
Smoke. I never got off on my right foot there. Maybe
I was lonesome for the old gang in 403. Maybe I was
in the wrong kind of atmosphere. Maybe it was myself. Probably that's the right answer. But by the time
I got out of there I was right back in the old lone wolf
frame of mind which I'd shucked off at OTU and in
403. That chip was on the shoulder again!

It certainly wasn't the squadron leader's fault, for
Nobby Fee, a Canadian who'd reverted from wingco
to SL to come overseas, was a swell fellow, always
sympathetic and understanding. I got along first rate
with the other Canucks in the outfit, Val Valiquette
from my own home town, Verdun, and Bob Middlemiss, who hailed from another Montreal suburb,
Westmount. Bob left for service overseas shortly after
I arrived. But not so with all the others. I wasn't at
outs with them, I simply wasn't in. Seemed to me they
were treating me like a kid fresh from OTU, not like
a guy with three or four months in a fighter squadron
at his back. Anyway the whole business stuck in my
crop.

I LET GO THE NEAREST THING TO A BURST THAT I COULD
FIRE—THE GUY SIMPLY BLEW UP

Nothing much happened for the first week—a couple of routine scrambles and a fighter sweep with Boulogne as its orbit. On the 26th I helped escort bombers to Le Havre and got a little action, but nothing to speak of, as we were flying the close escort position. We did another fighter sweep on the 28th and two on the 30th, all three over Calais, but got no action of any kind. Then came May Day and my day; May 1st, when I shot down my first Hun! But, Holy Godfrey, how close the bloody Huns came to getting me!

We were briefed in our own dispersal hut about nine in the morning and three wings met over Beachy Head about 9:30, to sweep over Calais. I was flying at Number Four in Blue Section. That made me "Blue Four."

The sweep went in over Calais once without encountering either flak or Jerries. We went out over the sea and swept in again at 24,000 feet. As we came over the city five Focke-Wulfs dived to cut me out from the tail-end position—and they did. The first burst put cannon shells through both my wings. I did a quick flick and headed up into the sun, but the Huns had seen me and followed. They had more speed than I, as they had just pulled out of a dive and they went right past me in the glare, going up. I pulled up sharply and took a bead on the one in the middle. By then he must have been about 300 yards away. The shots my own ship had taken had put my port guns out of action and my starboard cannon was practically dangling out of the wing. That left me with nothing but my two starboard machine guns. Anyway, I let go the nearest thing to a burst that I could fire and must have been covered with diamonds, for the guy simply blew up with a hell of an explosion. I must have copped him in the oxygen bottles. The wings fell

apart. The fuselage broke in two. The explosion must have killed the pilot, but the poor guy never had a chance to bale anyway. Right then and there the other four F-Ws legged for home—thank God. If they'd only known it, Beurling was a sitting bird right then. I could have been shot down with a water pistol.

I didn't waste a minute, but turned the nose straight for England. I was quite a piece in over France and the Spit was wallowing like a drunk. By the look of it the starboard wing was going to fall off any minute and Beurling would be floating down

under the silk, heading for a German prison camp—
if he was lucky enough to bale. But I was getting
there. Somehow the old Spitter and I stumbled across
the Channel and, boy! did those White Cliffs of Dover
ever look good! On the way in I phoned for the crash
wagon to meet me, for I was positive the Huns had
messed up my landing gear. But, believe it or not, the
cart went down and locked. The shots had missed it
by inches! As I came in to land the engine was streaming glycol and as soon as I stopped rolling bits and
pieces started to fall off and the glycol flowed out in a
torrent. Everything was overheated to hell and gone,
and if I'd had to fly another five minutes I'd have had
to bale and leave the crate to burn by itself. Oh, well,
I'd copped my first Jerry! That was something. But a
pretty sloppy show, none the less. Incidentally, that
was the only Hun shot down that day by the entire
RAF in Britain—and it was *not* done by deflection
shooting!

Squadron Leader Fee was on the field when I
came in and he shook my hand and said: "Nice going,
Beurling!" But up in mess that night a couple of guys
actually had the nerve to suggest that I'd got into
trouble because I'd broken formation. "Yair, that's
right," I said. "Six of us broke formation together—
five Jerries and I." I sure wasn't going to be very
happy around here. Nevertheless, I bagged me another
Hun on my very next sweep. That was May 3rd.

We were over the Calais area again, I carrying the tailboard as usual, when I spotted a squadron of Focke-Wulfs climbing up behind us. Apparently most of the crew thought they were Spitfires, but I called into the RT, "Aircraft climbing behind us are Focke-Wulf 190s," and some comedian replied: "Well, well! So they are!" Then Fee's voice came through, telling us to turn left and get around on their tails. That was all right as far as it went, but Jerry came into the mill making turns a good deal tighter than ours and I could see things mightn't be very happy, back in the Number Four slot, if I didn't watch out. Damned if I was going to be left carrying the baby again.

So I peeled off, all by my lonesome, and went into a steep dive, picking the Hun Leader and going right down onto him, off to starboard and letting him have a long burst from an angle—a deflection shot this time. He promptly went over into a vertical dive and went down trailing black smoke, shedding bits and pieces as he went. He was scored as a Probable at first. But three weeks later confirmation came through for a Destroyed, as he had been seen to hit the sea by a pilot low-flying with the rescue launch.

The other Jerries milled around for a minute or so after I'd popped their leader, but the party broke up quickly—and that was that. The squadron, meanwhile, had disappeared, so I headed for home, to find the others already there. Without ado a couple of the fellows started taking me to task for peeling off. I invited both of them to go jump at themselves and made for the orderly room to see the squadron leader.

"Look, sir," I said. "I've got to get out of here. I simply can't make it go with some of these fellows. Can I get a transfer?"

"You know what they're complaining about, Beurling," the CO replied. "You peeled off and left your Number Three's tail uncovered. That's not done, old man. Not around here!"

I pleaded guilty, but added that I figured I'd been left holding the bag on the previous sweep and nearly copped it as a result. I knew I was in the wrong, but, hell, I was angry about the whole thing.

"I know exactly how you feel," Fee said. "I'll see what can be done."

From that day forward life became progressively more stinking. Sweep after sweep I was left at home on the ground. Day after day I grew more and more angry, fed up, disgusted—pretty much like a spoiled kid, if you want to know.

I got in on one sweep on May 5th and two more on the 9th, but no serious action emerged from any, though we lost one Spitter and pilot on the 5th in a tangle with a handful of F-Ws over Saint-Omer. On the other two expeditions Jerry simply wouldn't play. That was my last taste of action with the squadron. It wasn't a very happy time for me. From the 9th to the 21st I spent a total of almost twelve hours in the air, every minute of it practice flying by myself. In the mess I was left pretty severely alone by my fellow pilots. Maybe they hadn't liked my individualistic tendencies, peeling off to go hunting alone. I don't blame 'em for that. Maybe they didn't like my way of talking straight from the shoulder—and I guess I was talking even straighter than usual about that time. Looking back from here, about the only comment I have to make is that I regret the fatheadedness, the lack of team spirit, that I showed. Not a very good show. I only hope the regrets are mutual as far as three or four other guys are concerned.

Then, Holy of Holies, I got the break I'd been praying for!

On the afternoon of the 21st one of our pilots was warned for posting overseas. The notice said the pilot "must be capable of taking off from an aircraft carrier." So you had a pretty fair idea that somebody was going someplace. In the mess I overheard the lad bewailing his fate. He was a bridegroom and things were like that, over to the house. Why did they pick on him to send abroad with a baby on the way? I pulled him over to one side. "Listen," I said, "if I get the orderly room to switch me into your place, would that be okay by you?"

Would it! The poor guy looked as if the Second Coming was right in the offing. So I hared for the orderly room and asked to see the CO. I put it up to him and he said: "I think I can fix it!" And, glory be, he did! The next day I left for the Embarkation Depot, where thirty-six pilots and about a hundred and fifty ground crew were being assembled. The day after arrival we were issued tropical kit and on the fourth day went aboard a merchantman. Below decks were thirty-six crated Spitfires! We sailed with the first tide, with one destroyer and a corvette as escort, bound for an unknown destination.

For the next week the air reeked with what are casually known as latrine rumors. We were going pretty nearly everywhere on the map, from Vladivostok to Moscow to Libya, with the accent on Libya. Practically nobody thought of Malta. We plowed steadily south, without sighting another ship all week. On the morning of the seventh day we made a landfall and by noon were in the harbor of Gibraltar. A couple of days later, after filling ourselves to the chins with fresh fruit, with huge steaks, and all the things none of us had tasted in months, after promenading half the night up and down brightly lighted streets and feeling like visitors from another world, we were informed that we'd be on our way to Malta in a matter of hours. The wing commander who gave us the news added: "And I can promise you plenty of fighting and a damned tough time!" That was no understatement.

Part Two

CHAPTER V

Malta

(ROBERTS: When Sergeant Beurling and his fellow reinforcement pilots and their Spitfires set out for Malta, the Mediterranean from Gib to Alexandria was a German-Italian lake. For well over fifteen hundred miles of water only a small ledge of rock seventeen miles long, nine in width, remained in British hands. Its great naval harbor at Valetta had long since been abandoned by the fleet, and small convoys, setting out to relieve siege conditions from Alex or the Rock, suffered 50 and 60 per cent casualties in their attempts to bring food and precious airplane fuel to the island. Manned by a handful of Spitfires, night fighters and bombers, Malta held out against the Hun, without relief, for endless months.

Its garrison had a job to do. That job was to harass Axis communications between the European mainland and North Africa and, on the African mainland, to hammer what was then Rommel's rear. The German and Italian Air Forces, for their part, were charged with the job of dislodging the defenders. Month in and month out, by day and by night, they plastered the island and its towns and villages with an unceasing hail of high-explosive and incendiary bombs. While other places along the United Nations' far-flung battlefront were withstanding two or three air raids a day and making world headlines, the Maltese people and their defenders were standing off a dozen German and Italian sorties in which the enemy came over from Sicilian airfields in battle formations a hundred planes strong. Thus month ' after month little Malta fought on, virtually unsung in its heroism.

What was the point of it all? Was it just cussedness on Britain's part, the determination to have no more Singapores? Certainly the defenders of the island must have wondered as they fought on, day after day, in the glaring Mediterranean sunlight, with no relief in sight. Then the tide turned. The Eighth Army broke through at El Alamein, shook itself into the clear and chased Rommel up the African coast. When it did so it possessed in Malta a base for aerial attack in the rear of the re-treating Afrika Korps and, as the enemy retreat became a runaway rout, a ready-made air base from which to pound the fleeing armies, on the one hand, and their sea communications, on the other. When the United Nations at last went on the offensive in North Africa, Malta was the key to Rommel's back door. Without Malta, Mont-gomery's task would have been infinitely more difficult.

Meanwhile, when Beurling and his fellow pilots set out from Gib in June, 1942, Malta without question was the hottest spot, from a fighter pilot's standpoint, in United Nations' hands. Pilots who fought in both battles rate the defense of Malta and the 'blitzing of its capital and its villages as a show even tougher than the Battle of Britain. As to that, let the record speak . . .)

Our arrival on that tiny piece of rock, in the center of a sea in which we hadn't a friend from Gib-raltar to Alexandria, was like coming awake from a pleasant dream into the heart of an earthquake. On the morning of June 7th, at Gib, thirty-two of us were

warned that we were to go aboard the aircraft carrier
Eagle that night and would sail on the morning of the
8th. That day everybody had a last fling ashore, a last
square meal, a last fill of fresh fruit.

Aboard ship the sergeant pilots snuggled down on
the steel deck below the flight deck, with nothing
between themselves and the hard metal but their
flying pants. But the view we had of the Rock as we
sailed through the Straits and into the blue Mediterranean next morning was common to all ranks. What
a sight! The flight deck of the small carrier was loaded
with our Spits and each of us was assigned to the baby
he would fly away tomorrow. Mine was 4196 and I
spent most of the day fussing around her and making
sure everything was okay for the flight ahead.

That night we were briefed by a wing commander, who told us that we would take off in flights
of eight and head due east until we picked up the jut
of the Tunisian coast. Then we would fly south by
east for a while and swing east again across the last
gap of water into Malta; about 745 miles in all, it
turned out to be. Each Spit carried two cannon,
loaded, but no machine guns, because room had to be
found in the wings for kit. Radio silence would be
maintained in flight for anything but *May Day*. We
could receive from the carrier and from Malta as we
approached the island.

"Keep your eyes peeled for Jerries as you come near home," the wing commander said. "The last time we came down this way the blighters lay in wait between Tunis and Pantelleria—a lot of people think he took off from that island—and shot down three or four Spitfires. Knocked every one of 'em into the sea and every pilot killed—just because he didn't keep his eyes peeled!"

Then he talked about carrier take-offs. We hadn't any too much room, he said. Open the throttle smoothly and quickly and hold her on the brake until she starts to buck and the tail tries to come up. Then give her the works and let her go. That's all. Good night.

By six o'clock next morning every pilot was at his station, ready to go. The *Eagle* was lying about fifty miles off the coast of Algeria, nose into wind and ready to turn in her tracks and run for Gib as soon as the Spitfires left her. The weather was cloudy but we were told to expect excellent visibility at Malta. By 6:05 the first eight were on the way, leaving the flight deck about two minutes apart. As each plane became airborne it climbed and made left-hand circuits of the carrier until joined by its mates. At 2,000 feet they formed up over the ship, then legged for Malta, climbing hard. I went away with the third flight at 6:30. Malta came into view at 9:50 from 20,000 feet. My

gang made Takali, all right side up, at 10:30. Right
then the war began in earnest for Sergeant Beurling!

I'll never forget the way we were told the score
the day we hit Malta, nor the things to be seen before
ever we scrambled over that beleaguered island. Malta
in 1942 was a siege, just as sure as Leningrad was a
siege, and the fact that the siege was being conducted

by air from Sicily made it no easier to take than if
Jerry had been just around the corner with his big
guns. After all, Sicily is only a block away from Malta
when you think in terms of today's flying speeds and
bomber loads.

We seemed to have blown right into the middle
of general hell from the azure peace of the western
Mediterranean. German and Italian fighters were up
there as we came in from the sea, waiting to pounce on
the newcomers, but kept away by the Malta Spits who

had gone up in a screen to protect us. Before the business of landing, checking in, finding quarters, and stowing your gear was finished you knew you had come to a war that was running twenty-four hours a day and you took at face value the words of the guy on the field at Takali, who told you just after you landed: "One thing about it here—you never have time to be scared!"

Bombs were liable to come whistling around your ears any minute. If you looked up you'd see Spits and Me's split-assing all over the sky and every once in a while some poor devil who hadn't kept his tail clean would come spinning down in flames. Flak went up in flowerbeds and parachutes came drifting down. From the ground the constant din of ack-ack batteries . . . Up high the clatter of machine-gun and cannon bursts and the roar of full-engined Spitfires, Me's and Macchis diving . . . Erks scurrying about the drome, patching bomb craters . . . Engineers detonating time bombs . . . Rescue launches rushing to sea to pick up floating parachutists . . . The Maltese population trying to carry on the day's chores between headlong dives for the shelter and protection of walls, cracked-up houses, or wrinkles in the rocks . . . Cats and dogs fighting in the streets in keeping with the tempo of the place . . . Never a dull moment, day or night. That was Malta in the blitzes. Before you

had been there a day you got the idea Jerry had decided to either sink the damned island or blow it away
—and you weren't far wrong.

If you'd had any remaining doubts they'd have
been removed by Wing Commander Gracey's brief
talk when he welcomed his new pilots to Takali. It
went something like this:

"By now you fellows know what you're up
against. You haven't come to a picnic and this is no
place for slackers. There isn't any tea in bed any more.
You've come to the place where the air fighting is
tougher than in any other corner of the war. You've
seen our fellows up there fighting and you've seen
some of them shot down while they were protecting
you, coming in. Tomorrow you may be up there and
you may get it. Day after tomorrow some of you may
be attending your own funerals if you don't keep your
eyes peeled. That's all. Good luck and good hunting!"

Great guy, the wingco. Tough. But what a prince,
and what a leader! Around Takali everybody said
Gracey had saved Malta from the Huns, nobody else.
Saved it by his spirit, by injecting that spirit into
everybody under his command, from pilots to erks.
(And, believe me, the erk is no slouch among warriors.
You ought to have seen him keep those Spits patched,
fueled, and flying at Malta, and you'd know he's the
real unsung hero of the show.) Every ground-crew man
on Takali adored Gracey, and no wonder. I hadn't

been on the drome a day before at least a dozen of them had let me know that I'd gone to work for Superman in person. "Blimy, sergeant," they'd say. "You'd ought to been 'ere the day Jerry dropped three bloody sticks on the plyce in one lump. We all ducked. 'Oo wouldn't? Abaht a minute later old Grycey is 'ere yelling like 'ell and wanting to know why the somethink-somethink nobody is on 'is job, and a lot more of the syme. Well, sergeant, next day Jerry 'its the field again and the wing commander is there when it 'appens and, blimy, if 'e don't duck just as 'ard and flat as anybody else. So what does 'e do? 'E 'as the 'ole bloody mob up on paride and makes a public apology! Now when Jerry comes everybody ducks, unless there's Spitfires to be moved . . . and no questions asked and no 'ell given. A real man, I'm telling you, sergeant, a real one, that one!"

Sure, he was tough. Malta's a tough place. Sure, he'd raise merry hell if one of his pilots cracked up a ship through some fool error, just as he did when Pilot Officer McElroy broke a Spitter's back in his first Takali landing. The wingco didn't realize then that Mac had hit his tail in getting away from the carrier. So Mac was grounded for his pains and came within an inch of being pushed on to the Middle East. Then the boss relented and Mac stayed on to become one of our first-rank fighter pilots. But a Spit was worth its weight in gold on Malta in June of '42, and to see one knocked off on arrival was too much of too much for any Jerry-ridden CO to bear, I guess. Blind as a bat, all the old-timers said Gracey was, but he couldn't be kept out of the air, particularly when the going was tough. Eleven Huns and Eyeties were his bag up to the time I hit Malta. A grand man, that was Wing Commander Gracey, a man in a spot that was always tough and who did his judging by results, not form.

We spent the 9th of June getting settled in quarters, each according to his rank, and in meeting the gang who would be our sidekicks and dogfight mates during the months ahead. Some of them I would see go spinning down out of control or in flames, before many days were gone. Others would be wiping Jerries off my own tail for me. It would always be a changing gang, but always a good one. These were faces a man would carry with him to the end of the trail.

I was assigned to 249 Squadron, proud of its record as the fightinest outfit in the RAF, with 180 German and Italian aircraft in its bag when I joined, and plenty more to come. Mostly we were Canadians, but Britain, the States, Australia, and New Zealand were always on hand as well. The squadron leader was Grant, a swell Englishman and a swell pilot, who was still around Malta when I hit the silk in October, thought not flying, and at Luqa, not Takali. The flight commanders were Laddie Lucas and Buck McNair, English and Canadian, both top-drawer guys and the latter one of the greatest fighter pilots the RAF ever owned. McNair left Malta ·soon after I arrived, with eight Destroyeds and a fistful of Damageds and Probables in his kit. Among the commissioned pilots were Norm Lee, Daddo-Langois (Daddy Longlegs to everybody in 249) and Berkeley-Hill, all Englishmen; Jonesy Jones, Al Yates, and Mac Mac-Lean, Canadians. Chuck Ramsay, who held warrant officer's rank, was another Canuck, and so were Sergeants John Williams (Willie the Kid), de Nencrede, Micky Butler, and Bob Middlemiss, who had come out a month earlier from 41. Paul Brennan and Gil Gilbert came from England and Australia; Heslin and Rae were New Zealanders—the last four all sergeants.

A whole mob of reinforcement pilots for the Fighting 249th had arrived with me from Gib and the *Eagle,* for this was strictly an expendable outfit. Jean Paradis, a swell French-Canadian kid from Shawinigan Falls, Quebec, talked a broken English that was a joy to the outfit. (His last words, spoken over the RT at 20,000 feet, at the beginning of his last dogfight were "I see the bom-bairs. I go there!" Poor old Jean. Many the dogfight and many the swim we enjoyed together!) Harry Kelly, our only Yank, was a Texan and a real deep-in-the-heart-of guy. McElroy and Lattimer, both

officers, were from England and New Zealand. Of the
new flock of sergeant pilots Baxter was Aussie, Tommy
Tompkins, Louis de l'Ara and Ernie Budd were English, Rip Mutch and myself were Canadians. That
was 249, as I first got to know it around the dispersal
hut on June 9, 1942—a grand, if sometimes screwy,
outfit. Remember those names. You'll be hearing
more of them. A lot of those sergeants are officer pilots
now, still flying Spits. A lot of the gang have knocked
down more than their share of Huns and Eyeties since
then. Not many of them were on Malta when I left,
because three or four months of that inferno are about
all a pilot can take—if he lives that long. And a lot
of those grand fellows aren't around anywhere any
more—which is something you don't talk about
around dispersal, waiting for the next scramble, nor
in mess, when you're loafing.

We weren't the only fighter mob on Malta, not
by a jugful. If we had been there wouldn't be *any* of
us around to tell the tale, or any Malta left in our
hands to tell about, I guess. There were other Spitfires on Takali with us, more at Luqa, and more again
at Halfar. There were big bombers around too, the
lads who pestered Rommel's supply lines. There were
the night fighters (they say Moose Fumerton, a
Canadian, who flew Beaufighters over Malta, is the
best night-fighter pilot in the RAF!), torpedo planes
and some other odds and ends. We didn't see much of

them in the Spitter outfits. We had one job to do and
that was to defend a hunk of bald rock, seventeen
miles long by nine wide, from an enemy who was
determined to blow it to hell. We hadn't time for
anything else. Even when we weren't flying (and I had
arrived at the fag end of a blitz, just before a lull) we
were always on call, always waiting for Jerry.

How did we live? What did we eat? The sergeant
pilots lived comfortably enough in a huge private
home. We ate in another house near by, with bar and
lounge in the same building. The food was siege grub:
bully beef, bully beef, and more bully beef in innumerable disguises, but still bully. For fresh vegetables we had the pick of the home crop, grown in the
thinnest but most highly fertilized soil in the world.
A good Malta cabbage probably nourishes a man. In
addition it breaks him out in a pimply rash and gives
him Malta Dog, which is dysentry's first cousin—and
was everybody's semipermanent boarder. You didn't
live on Malta. You got by and made the best of it and
shot down all the Jerries you could, while you could.

At Malta you'd get Jerries by going up and potting them, man to man. No more of these beautifully
executed fighter sweeps which had been my introduction to operations over Britain and France, where you
could be pretty nearly shot at dawn for breaking out
of formation and peeling off to chase a Hun. No more
massed wings of Spitfires, maybe two hundred strong,

FO G. F. Beurling with rudder and unit insignia from a Macchi C.202 shot down by him over Gozo Island 1942. (Imperial War Museum)

Top
Spitfire Vs of 249 Squadron on Takali Airfield Malta summer 1942. (D. H. Newton/
R. L. Ward)

Middle
Macchi C.202 crash landed on Gozo 1942. This is an aircraft of 378ª Squadriglia,
155° Gruppo. (Imperial War Museum)

Bottom
Spitfire Vc of 229 Squadron (BR 553) flown by Squadron Leader M. M. 'Mike'
Stephens when he was serving as a supernumerary with 229 Squadron in late summer
1942. (M. Stephens/R. C. Jones)

Top
A pair of Spitfire Vs from the Takali Wing in flight. The furthest aircraft is from 249 Squadron, while that closest to the camera is believed to be serving with 229 Squadron. (R. C. Jones)

Bottom
Squadron Leader Stephens' Spitfire Vc BR 553 following a crash landing. (M. Stephens/R. C. Jones)

Top
Army personnel with bicycles and a group of R.A.F. pilots around Wg Cdr P. P. Hanks' Spitfire Vc. (R. C. Jones)

Bottom
A group of Malta fighter pilots sitting in front of a pair of aircraft representative of the units based at Takali. In the background is a Beaufighter strike aircraft of 272 Squadron while in front of this is a Spitfire Vc flown by the Takali Wing Leader Peter Prosser Hanks; the aircraft carries his initials PP-H.
3rd from left Wg Cdr J. K. Buchanan (272 Sqdn), 4th from left Sqdn Ldr M. M. Stephens (229 Sqdn). (R. C. Jones)

escorting half a dozen Bostons to lay a few eggs on Ostend or Comines. Here it was the other way around. Here it was Jerry who came over in mass sweeps, with clouds of fighters to escort the JU 88s while they took another sock at poor old Malta. Then it would be "Scramble Red Section!" or "Scramble Four Aircraft!" and maybe Willie the Kid, Jonesy, Harry Kelly, and Daddy Longlegs would be out of the all-day poker game in dispersal, running to their Spits like bats out of hell. Or if it was something pretty special, maybe all 249 Squadron would be scrambled. Then card tables would go over like ninepins, cards and cash would hit the floor, pilots would jam the doorway, and guys would even be baling out the windows to get to those aircraft and up at those Huns. You'd grind up there to meet them as if the fate of mankind depended on the time you could make in reaching 20,000 feet and picking yourself a handful of Jerries and Eyeties with odds of five, seven, and even ten to one against you. That was Malta for the Spit pilots that summer—a full-time job, in doing which you were quite likely to be reading a book, drinking a cup of chocolate, or trying to figure how to bet three aces one minute and halfway off the grasstops the next, waiting for Ops to tell you where to go and what you might expect when you got there. One sure bet you always had—when you met the other fellows you could be sure there'd be more of him than of you, considerably more.

Operations hung out "down in the ditch," which is underground, deep beneath the island's rocks, in ordinary language. Down there they knew on the instant what trouble might be shaping up over Sicily, and could send us out telling us just what to expect and where to do our expecting. Then we'd be away, always shorthanded, because there was never enough gas to do any fooling. You play for keeps when you're holding an island pinpoint, entirely surrounded by your enemies, with nothing but the occasional pint-size convoy getting through with fuel and food every now and then—and plenty of ships going down on the way.

You would do a lot of wondering about the why of it, particularly after some sidekick you thought a lot of had gone down and hit the deck. Why would anybody in his senses want to hang onto a hunk of rock, so exposed that not even the navy could use it? Why didn't we just get the hell out of there and let Jerry have the damned place if he wanted it? Why didn't we just tell the Malties to keep it and go on home? After a while you knew why, but you didn't get it at first, and sometimes you were convinced it was all screwy. Then you realized that just so long as the fighter pilots could hang on and keep knocking the Me 109s and the Macchis and the Ju 88s into the sea we still had a toehold in the Mediterranean and an advance base close to the African coast that the other fellows couldn't use as a jumping-off place. And when you lay back on the hospital pillows, thousands of miles away from Malta, when Montgomery and the Eighth Army came rolling up the coast from Egypt, chasing Rommel and the Afrika Korps back to Tripoli and beyond, you realized at last that not one of those grand guys you'd lived and fought with from Kalfrana Bay to the Sicily coast had spun down in vain. Malta had played a superhuman role in keeping the stage set for the Big Show—and the lads who went west in the Spits had done a great part of the job.

So this was the place I'd come to, after traipsing all over hell's half-acre looking for a spot where a Spitfire pilot could get some action—a hunk of bald rock in the middle of the sea, a hunk of bully beef swimming in grease—a job liable to begin with a hurry-up call from bed at 2:30 in the morning and not end until the sun went down over toward Gib, where the lights would be shining and the bars and cafes crowded with laughing men and girls. The pay-off was the job you had to do, but even more than that it was the guys you did the job with. What is written from now on is for them. . . .

Jerry was in high spirits in those days. Well he might be, for he had been giving the aerial defenders of Malta a rough ride and the island itself a terrific pounding. Almost my first recollection of the place, in fact (and I think it was on my first day of duty, June 10th), is of seeing a trio of Me 109s come whipping down out of nowhere and go frisking across the field at Takali no more than ten feet off the ground, doing rolls and helling around generally, then twisting back and shooting the joint up, like a bunch of horse-opera cowboys going to town. This was a new kind of Jerry, not the fellow I'd tangled with around Occupied France. "Saucy lot of bastards, aren't they?" That was Willie the Kid's phrase for the visitors as they raced back out to sea, heading for Sicily.

I didn't get off the ground until the 11th, when a four-man scramble turned out to be nothing but a routine patrol, the raiders turning back before reaching the island. We made no attempt to follow. Gas was at a premium right then, and would be until the next convoy came through.

On the 12th I got my first real feel of Malta action. I was in Red Section that morning, and Red is always first off, just an old Air Force custom, I guess. We had been aroused at four o'clock and at half past the bus was outside our sleeping quarters waiting to take us to the field. From then until about seven we sat around the dispersal hut, drinking hot chocolate and talking. Then the phone rang and Ops sang out, "Scramble Four aircraft!" and we were away, Daddy Longlegs, Berkeley-Hill, Jack Rae, and I—off the

HE WENT DOWN VERTICALLY—NOBODY SAW HIM HIT THE
DECK, SO I WAS CREDITED WITH A DAMAGED

ground in a few seconds over the minute. That's the way the scrambles moved on Malta!

Almost as soon as we were airborne the orders came over the RT: "Gain angels as quickly as possible!" We did. "Angels" being RAFese for altitude, those four Spitfires went up the big hill together like dingbats and were at 18,000 feet in something better than ten minutes. There Ops came in again: "Party of fifteen enemy aircraft, boys, coming in from Zonkor Point at twenty-one to twenty-two thousand. No big jobs." That's "no bombers" to you. It meant that four Spitfires were commissioned to take on almost four times their own number of Me's and probably Italian Macchis, pretty much the usual odds in that gas-starved country.

We flew line abreast, as we always flew at Malta, the better to watch each other's tails. The Jerries came down to the attack, peeling off in pairs and diving, after sending down one lone Messerschmitt as decoy. Then the melee started. The Me's split us and Berkeley-Hill and I found ourselves alone. About four Jerries jumped B-H and as they did I pulled up sharply under one and blew his tail off. He went down vertically and that was the last I saw of him. Nobody saw him hit the deck, but Berkeley-Hill had seen my burst hit, so I was credited with a Damaged.

Meanwhile Jack Rae had tangled with another Hun and pumped lead into him—another Damaged.

Daddy Longlegs had tried a head-on attack on an Me
and picked up a few bullet holes in his own wings for
his trouble. We were all milling around like madmen,
the four of us trying to keep our own and each other's
tails clean and at the same time maneuver Jerries into
our sights. After about ten minutes the visitors decided to call the whole thing off, put their noses down
and high-tailed toward Sicily. Thirty-five minutes
after hearing the Scramble Call we were all down
again on Takali. That was my first taste of action over
the Mediterranean. It had added one Damaged to my
meager bag from France, but it had done something
more than that—in those brief moments of combat I
had proved, to myself, that I had the stuff to match
flying and shooting with the gentlemen from Sicily.
That is what I had wanted to find out, and find out in
a hurry. As we walked away from our Spits, Daddy
Longlegs grinned at me and said: "Good show,
Beurling!" I felt swell.

Right then the luck soured and 249 was grounded
for ten solid days while its Spitfires were taken apart
and put together again. To the old-timers the break
was more than welcome. While the other squadrons
looked after the business of keeping an eye on the
enemy (actually the lull was on in earnest, the Hun
needing a chance to rest and refit every bit as much as
we did—only he, as attacker, was the chooser of time),
they could slip away to the RAF Hostel down the coast

to rest ragged nerves and catch up on much-needed sleep in the only place on the island where a man could find a decent meal. And how some of those guys needed the break! You get pretty twitchy when life consists of a series of weeks of sudden calls to scramble, interspersed with hours of sitting in a hut waiting to be called on instant notice, to be off in a minute. I remember one veteran of the Maltese blitzes (and the Malta Dog, I'll bet!), a fellow soon to be one of my best pals and flying partners, to whom I made some simple, sap observations my first or second day on the island. The guy looked at me as if I had walked in on his dearest privacy. "For Christ's sake, can't you keep quiet?" he barked, and slammed out of the room. In my greenness I decided I'd bumped into a Number One boor. What I didn't know was that he'd seen two of his best friends shot down during a scramble only a couple of days before I hit Malta, and had been powerless to help them. For the time being he wanted no part of anybody's company.

Plenty of courageous people get the twitch under the constant drive of the other fellow's blitz—and Louis de l'Ara, who'd seen both, always said the going was tougher on Malta than it had been in the Battle of Britain. I wouldn't know, and I'm starting no arguments. Malta was tough enough for anybody; let it stand at that. The occasional betwitched pilot may take to the bottle, but very few do. You won't find many who didn't learn long ago that you can't keep your tail clean while you're nursing a hangover. Some get moody. Some pick quarrels with everybody they meet. Some lose confidence and brood about the law of averages. And when people like Wing Commander Gracey see the symptoms, the victim gets a rest or, if he's been around for long, a trip to Gib and England on leave.

So the ten-day layoff looked like heaven to most of the old-timers of 249. But to a green youngster like me, who had tasted one brief day of battle, and pined for more, it was a time of restless stomping around, praying for something to do. I'd watch the German and Italian sweeps come over and the Spits from the other outfits up there trading lead with them and I'd say to myself: "You'll never get chances like this again!" Willie the Kid and Bob Middlemiss would look at me and say: "Hold your fire, big boy. You'll get your chance. Don't worry. Everybody gets it here, automatically. You don't have to go looking for it!"

Somehow the days passed. During them Jean Paradis and I got to know each other better by slipping off to Siliema to swim and lie in the sun on the smooth white rocks. I guess it was Willie the Kid who introduced me to the adjacent island of Gozo, less than half the size of Malta and, of all things, neutral. You could slip across the narrow gut of water, past Comino, and on Gozo find a decent steak to eat. Once or twice I made the trip to the rest house, just for the day. But mostly I hung around the drome, watching the erks at work on my Spit. Then I'd sneak up the hill to my room and lie around boning up the text-books and working out pet theories of deflection shoot-ing on paper. What I needed was action. And pretty soon I got it!

The 23rd saw us back in the air, with just one scramble, which went pfft before it ever got going. Ops had given us plenty of warning of whatever was shap-ing up over Sicily and by the time the sweep ap-proached Malta we had more height than Jerry and were waiting for him. He turned tail for home. Mostly Jerry is built that way. He'll run and fight another day when the odds don't look good to him. The Eye-ties, on the other hand, will stay and fight it out far oftener than the Germans will.

No action on the 24th, but plenty the next day. A mob of us scrambled to meet a big Jerry fighter sweep early in the morning and walked into a hell of a mess of dogfighting. I'd never seen a brawl like it before. We were all over the sky, everybody trying to keep out of trouble and draw a bead on somebody else. Aircraft were chasing each other around in tight turns like cats in an alley. That was the show in which poor Harry Kelly connected, right before the big mix-up began. He'd been feeling like hell for days—a touch of the Dog, I guess—but wouldn't go sick and wouldn't beg off. Getting into action he had lagged out of formation for a moment and some watchful Hun had spotted him and dived. Over the RT I heard somebody yell Harry's identification call and: "Enemy aircraft diving out of the sun! Break left!" But the call came too late and one short burst got him.

We had no luck on that scramble, but we were up again before noon to meet a mixture of German and Italian fighters, about thirty of them, escorting three Cant bombers. We turned the Cants back and made them drop their bombs in the sea and most of the fighters stuck around and tangled awhile. My four, led by Mac MacLean, were detailed as cover and didn't get into the real mill, in which Lattimer knocked off one Me, got a Probable for another and damaged one of the Cants. The sky was full of tracer while the show lasted. It would have been rated a good party, but bad luck was dogging 249 that day. Tommy Tompkins's Spit was pretty badly shot up and he was hit in the engine and radiator. He pulled out of the mix-up and tried to make Takali, instead of going over on his back and baling. At that he nearly made it. He came in over the island streaming glycol and trying his damnedest to stretch his glide. He cut it too fine and suddenly flicked into a spin at 150 feet, bursting into flames as he hit the ground.

We were called again for still another show, this time to provide escort for the High Seas Rescue

Launch which had gone out to pick up a couple of lads from one of the other Spitfire outfits who had baled into the sea during one of the afternoon dog-fights. Willie the Kid and I teamed for this chore, hanging around between 5,000 and 10,000 feet to make sure no Jerries horned in while the boys were being fished out of the drink and brought home. Boy! How those rescue launches go to town when the *May Day* call comes in! And how the lads in the parachutes and the rubber dinghies need that help and protection! To the gentle Hun the only good enemy pilot is a dead pilot. Of which more later.

After all the action of the 25th we green hands thought the new blitz had begun. But the old-timers pooh-poohed such twaddle. "The Hun's only feeling us out," they said. "When he really begins you'll know he's begun. Just wait." Actually we didn't so much as get a smell of a Hun for the next couple of days. Then on the 28th four of us got in a good harrier run with eight or nine Me's. We chased each other around the sky for an hour, but never so much as got into range. Just fighters, no big jobs. Our friends were out looking for information, not trouble. The 29th was all quiet. On the 30th twenty-five German and Italian fighters came over on a look-see sweep and eight of us scrambled for forty minutes before we turned them back. Lattimer and Berkeley-Hill's aircraft were shot up during the proceedings and each had to make a crash landing. Both were shaken up, but both were back in dispersal next morning, complete with Mae Wests. If a ruckus suddenly started we might need all the pilots we could scrape up.

The end of June found the lull so thick you could slice it, the kind of lull that hangs over your head on a thread and may brain you any minute. We all knew the muck would go off with a bang without warning. Everybody had the jitters, because it was Jerry who would choose the time for the earthquake, not the defenders of Malta, who could only wait, take it when it came, and try to hand it back double. Conversation around the poker table was getting pretty hard to take. Nobody liked the way his fellow players dealt the cards, or shuffled them, or made their bets. Close buddies were beginning to snap at each other. Laughs were fewer and came harder. What can be tougher than to be forced to sit in a hole waiting for somebody to drop a brick on your head? Well, that was Malta in the Big Lull!

The Huns and the Eyeties stayed away all through the first four days of July. Night bombings were away below par. But on the 5th seven Ju 88s sneaked through and dropped a flock of delayed-action bombs on the field at Takali. The fellows who had gone up to intercept were hurriedly told by Ops to land at Luqa. Those of us who were at home

scrambled pronto in the same direction. We got everything out before a bomb exploded.

There could be only one answer to that. Jerry was
coming after us at last and trying to knock us out on
the ground before he started. Swell. It was a much
happier gang which bussed from Luqa to the Takali
pilots' quarters that night to catch a few brief hours of
sleep. The tension was off. People began to grin at
each other again. As for Beurling—Well, I'd been on
Malta almost a month and had exactly one Damaged
to show for it. About time something happened!

CHAPTER VI

Hell Lets Loose

By eight o'clock on the morning of July 6th eight of us were racing for 22,000 feet to intercept a raid of three Cant bombers and thirty fighters, headed for Luqa for the same purpose for which the Ju's had visited Takali the day before—to knock us out on the ground.

The first job was to turn back those Cants, no matter what else happened, so we promptly crashed through the fighter screen to get at the bombers. We met them head-on before they reached the island and by the grace of God and eight Spitfires stopped them in their tracks and made them unload in the sea. The bombers didn't get off scot-free just by dropping their bombs in the Mediterranean, however. Smith knocked one full of holes and it was last seen limping away toward Sicily. I got a two-second angle shot in on another and could see cannon shells and machine-gun bullets pepper his fuselage. Later we heard through Intelligence that the pilot had been killed and that the observer had flown the wounded crew home to a crash landing. Two out of three Cants Damaged; one for Smitty, one for me. At least they hadn't laid their eggs on Luqa. Now for the fighters!

As the bombers turned to run I saw a Macchi 202 boring in on Smitty's tail. I did a quick climbing turn and bored in on the Eyetie, catching him unawares. A one-second burst smacked him in the engine and glycol tank. He burst into flames and went down like a plummet. The same performance followed with another Macchi. Like the first one this baby picked on

Smitty, and I on Smitty's friend. He saw me coming, however, and broke away diving. We went down vertically together from 20,000 to about 5,000 feet and I let him have it just as he pulled out, from about 300 yards and slightly to starboard. God knows where I hit him but he exploded into a million pieces. Number Two.

As I pulled out and started to climb back up to the main dogfight I saw a lad go into the sea in flames about two miles south of my own position and was able to confirm him for Norm Lee—Norm's third Destroyed and his first Flamer. Al Yates, who had followed me down thinking I was hit, was able to confirm my second Macchi, and Lee had seen both of them. So there was my confirmation for two Destroyed. Yates's own ship was bullet-riddled and Al had to make a dead-stick landing, but escaped unscathed.

By then the enemy was ready to call it a sweep and go home. As we turned back from the sea Ops called to tell us to land on our own drome, where the Bomb Demolition Squad had tidied up the mess. When I hopped out of the cockpit I discovered my own Spitter pretty well perforated in the wings and fuselage and couldn't for the life of me remember where I'd picked the stuff up. Sloppy work, somewhere! Anyway it had been a pretty good show when you figure we were only away thirty-five minutes. We had knocked off three Macchis and damaged two

Cants, against two Spits damaged, Al's and mine. In that short mix-up my own Malta score had stepped up to two Destroyed and two Damaged. Things were looking up. You can pack a lot of action into half an hour when you get on the beam.

I had learned something else on that flip, something I'd often heard but never seen. It was the Macchis, the Eyeties, who came in and mixed it with us, not the Messerschmitts. All through the party the Huns had sat up high, looking for cold meat to pounce on, but keeping the hell out of the fracas. It was like that a good part of the time. The Jerries are probably better over-all pilots than the Italians, but they certainly let the Eyeties do their fighting for them when the going got tough. When we get around to adding up the final score for this show I hope somebody thinks of that.

As soon as the Spits were refueled we were scrambled again, but this time the raid turned back and we simply patrolled the island for forty-five minutes at about 27,000 feet. In the early afternoon I was called to fly cover patrol for the rescue launch which went out to pick up the two Italian pilots I had shot down in the morning. One died that night in hospital, badly burned. The other had been hit in the leg by a cannon shell and in the shoulders and arms with machine-gun bullets. The doc had to amputate the leg. The pilot lived.

Just before sunset Willie the kid, Daddy Long-legs, Norm Lee, and I scrambled to take on two Ju 88s escorted by about twenty Me 109Fs. Willie and Daddy went in for the bombers and Norm and I went on up to occupy the fighters' attention. As we did, two Me's dropped on me, but I did a quick wing-over and got onto one's tail. He saw me coming and tried to climb away. I figured he must be about 800 yards away from me when I got him in the sights and let go at him. It was a full deflection shot, and I had to make plenty of allowance for cannon-drop. I gave him a three-second burst, smack on his starboard flank, and got him in the glycol tank. He started to stream the stuff, leaving a long white trail of smoke. His partner, thinking better of it all, legged for Sicily. I followed my man down almost to sea level, where he burst into flames and went into the drink—must have overheated from loss of so much glycol.

I turned then and began to look for the other lads; instead, I spotted two Me's way down low, flying toward Sicily. I gave chase and followed them to within five miles of the coast, but they got away. On the return trip I saw one of the Ju's, escorted by two Me's, flying home low over the water, a favorite trick when you're homing and not anxious to let anybody get in under you. As I started to drop toward them I saw two other Messerschmitts and decided against tangling, as my ammunition was nearly all gone and

I'd be running short of gas if I stayed and fooled around. So I high-tailed across the sea for Malta, letting down pretty close to the water. About four miles short of the coast I turned and saw two Spits trailing about a thousand yards behind me, something no friendly guy is supposed to do. Your pals fly out to one side, where you can see them, not in your blind spots. So I thought: "I'll just show these birds I have my eyes peeled." I pulled into a quick climbing-turn and damned if the two Spits didn't fire on me! Cripes! I was mad—until I saw the two Spits pass under me. Lo and behold! My two "pals" were Messerschmitts. They had seen me tailing the bomber and had tailed me home, hoping for a cold-meat shot. The failing light had fooled me completely! That was something else to remember for the rest of time. Just for hellry I took a pot shot at the rear Me, but the light was too low for any kind of sighting, so I slipped in across the coast and dropped down on Takali.

My big mill had happened in full view of the island and everybody had seen my Me go out to sea streaming glycol. A few minutes after I landed Willie the Kid came home and said he had seen the lad go into the sea. So that made my score for the day: three Destroyed (two Macchis and one Messerschmitt) and one Damaged (the Cant).

Nobody else had any luck on the sunset scramble. Norm Lee had been chasing fighters all over hell-and-

gone and had tried a couple of bursts, without result.
Willie and Daddy had pursued the bombers across the
sea and then had come back to look for the dogfight,
but by that time the melee was broken up and they
hadn't been able to find any action.

That was July 6th. The Big Blitz was on!

(ROBERTS: "Wait a minute, George," I said. "A couple
of questions here. First: This was your first big bag. How
did you feel . . . on top of the world, weary, let down,
how?" Buerling said he felt fine, not tired, not anything
particularly special, just all right. "But wait a minute,"
I countered. "You must have felt elated, at least, by the
day's success!" No, he hadn't felt elated, the young man
answered. At least not so far as he could remember. After
all, he'd always known he could shoot 'em down with
these deflection angles he had practiced until he was black
in the face. All he had ever needed was the chance. The
answer wasn't cocky, nor was it modest. Just the plain
matter-of-fact reply of a fellow who knew; a perfectionist's
answer. The other question was: "What about the other
fellows, after you landed from the last scramble? Did they
gang you with congratulations? Did they throw a party
for you that night in the mess?" "Hell, no," said George.
"What was there to throw a party about? I guess Gracey
said something about 'Good work, Beurling.' But we
never did run around kissing guys when they shot Jerry
down. That was the idea. That was what we were in Malta
for. You were much more likely to thank the guy who
had wiped a Hun off your tail than to make a lot of bother
about his personal scores.")

Both sides were glad to take it easy on the 7th
. . . plenty of bullet holes to patch. But soon after

daylight on the 8th the Jerries were back, throwing everything but the kitchen sink at us. Seven Ju 88 bombers escorted by forty Messerschmitts were all we were offered—Smitty, Gilbert, Willie the Kid, and I. Thank God we got a little help before we had been up there long! From the Spitter guys at Halfar, seems to me.

The scramble call had come a bit late, with the result that the Huns were over the island at 18,000 while we were still at 12,000 on the way up to meet them. The Messerschmitts came down on us in a cloud, so we never got near the Junkers, which dive-bombed the Takali field, but missed, letting most of their stuff go into the near-by village of Attard. The Messerschmitts chased us all over Malta, the yellow-nosed bastards! You were flying in tracer smoke all the time and it seemed you would never get a chance to pick yourself an opponent. There were so many of them they kept you too damned busy watching your own tail. Finally I got one guy into my sights, from the tail, just for an instant. I let him have a two-second burst. He began to pour black smoke and hit the sea about three miles south of Gozo. Two of the Halfar lads saw him go in and he was confirmed as Destroyed.

The scrap was short but sweet. Smitty had tried to bore in on the bombers, all on his lonesome and about twenty Me's leaped after him. Smitty must have decided it was too hot (who wouldn't?), for he whipped around in a hell of a hurry and surprised the whole pack by dashing in under them and streaking for home and mother. The Jerries gave chase, and that broke up the main mix-up. Meanwhile Gilbert and Willie the Kid were milling around in the mess of Huns, each trying to pick one for himself. Neither had any luck, but each came home with his ship riddled like a sieve. "Jesus! that was hot while it lasted," said Willie, as we ambled back to dispersal. Hot is right. Yet we were off the ground only twenty-five minutes, not a second more!

The second scramble of the day seemed to open in highly favorable circumstances, yet it ended tragically, costing 249 two of its best pilots. Again the visitors consisted of seven Ju 88 bombers, heavily escorted by fighters. We had much more warning than for the earlier mix-up and there were more of us to handle the job. But somehow it didn't come off right.

Eight of us scrambled together: Smitty, Gilbert, Willie the Kid, Heslin, Berkeley-Hill, Micky Butler, Daddy Longlegs and myself. We were ready and waiting for the Ju's at 25,000 feet as they came in over Malta at 14,000. The lot of us dived vertically, hitting between 550 and 600 miles an hour down the hill. I wanted to get a bomber, so I picked the one on the starboard flank and went down on him through the screen of fighters. As I came in on him, leveling off, I gave him the works on a deflection angle right in the starboard engine, which burst into flames. What happened to him after that I didn't know, because right then five Messerschmitts came at me from as many corners of the compass. I dogfought the whole bunch, trying my damnedest to line one up in the sights without exposing myself to the others, and finally got one where I wanted him. I gave him a quick burst while I had him there and his engine took fire. He was last seen diving vertically toward Filfola Island, three miles south of Malta. The other Me's cleared out.

So far, so good. But while all this was going on, Smitty and Gil had picked out a couple of bombers and were really going to town on the boys, breaking down through the high fighters as if they weren't there, and boring in for the kill. At least fifteen Messerschmitts promptly came diving down to the bombers' help and nailed Smitty and Gil when the rest of us were busy elsewhere and didn't even know what was happening. Smitty took fire on the first burst. Two more Me's bored in and pasted him again (I suppose each of the bastards wanted part-credit for the kill!), blowing his Spit to bits and giving Smitty no chance to bale, if he was still alive. The same gang got Gil in the same second of sudden death. He simply went over on his back and fell headlong into the sea.

Willie the Kid came close to hearing harps that morning. For Willie had broken through the fighters with the rest of us to pick out a Ju, which caught fire from the port gas tank as soon as Willie put a burst into him. Willie was always a lad to get a great bang out of everything and he stuck around to watch his Flamer go down, about as foolish, if human, a thing a guy can do, because a flaming aircraft attracts attention all over the sky and brings all sorts of unwanted people around. When I spotted the Kid he was flying around his burning bomber, seeing the sights and completely oblivious to three Me's hovering over him, waiting to pounce. Believe me, I went in fast on those Schmitts, head on, the only way I could take their attention away from the blue-plate lunch Willie was setting up for them. As I came whipping in they broke upwards. I didn't get a chance to put a burst into any of them; they beat it so fast. Anyway, Willie's tail was tidy again!

"For Christ's sake, Willie," I said as we walked away from our Spits on the 'drome, "will you keep your eyes peeled?" Willie laughed. "Wasn't he a beaut?" "Who do you think *I* am?" I asked. "Your mother?" "Hi, mom!" said Willie. Then we walked in together and heard about Gil and Smitty . . .

The Ju which nearly cost the Kid his own life was definitely a Destroyed. Heslin had copped another, last seen trailing smoke near the sea. All Hes got for that was a Probable, however, as nobody saw the Jerry hit the water. Micky Butler had seen my Ju heading out to sea with one engine afire, so that was rated a Damaged. The Me I sent diving aflame over Filfola was counted as a Probable, as no one saw him go in, though various people reported they could plainly see the spot where an aircraft had hit the sea. That meant the squadron had scored one Destroyed, one Damaged, and two Probables, for which we had traded two of our real solid guys in Smitty and Gil. In addition Micky Butler barely got home with his ship shot to ribbons. Not one of our better mix-ups. Things were pretty gloomy around home that night. We were all damned glad when Jerry took the next day off to lick his own wounds.

The 10th was another all-out day, during which Malta's Spitfires stood off half a dozen enemy raids. 249 took part in three of these shows.

The first came early in the morning and sixteen pilots got the call, eight from Luqa and four each from Takali and Halfar. McElroy, Lattimer, Rae and I were the 249 quartette. Our opponents were four Ju 88s escorted by thirty Messerschmitts. The Luqa and Halfar lads knocked off three bombers. We drew the job of attending to the top-escort fighters. It was the old story of few against many, which means you split up and go hunting around until you can pick yourself a spot to get a Jerry, at the same time trying to keep out of harm's way. Most of the forty minutes we were up were spent in milling around, trying to come to grips, and every one of us finally drew blood. Jack Rae's ship was badly shot up, but Jack destroyed an Me. McElroy got another. Lattimer added a Macchi to his tally and I had the good fortune to bump into a Hun who forgot to keep his eyes peeled while he was getting ready to dive on one of our guys. All I had to do was to dive on him quickly, pull up sharply and to starboard as I got under him, and put a burst into his belly. The squirt must have killed the pilot. The ship didn't catch fire. No bits and pieces flew off. I saw no oil or glycol smoke. One second he was in my sights. The next he was diving headlong for the Mediterranean! In addition to destroying three Junker bombers, the Luqa and Halfar lads picked up another Probable bomber and Destroyed two fighters. That made nine Jerries and Eyeties Destroyed, plus a Probable, in little more than half an hour! Nine of 'em down. For Smitty and Gil!

The second scramble was a thirty-plus affair . . . a mixture of Messerschmitts and Macchis and five bombers. The Messerschmitts were flying close escort for the Ju's and the Macchis were top cover. Sixteen Spitfires were sent to meet them, eight from 249. I remember this show particularly because it was the first time I flew with Eric Hetherington, just transferred to our mob from one of the other Spitfire squadrons to replace Smitty. Hether was a Yorkshireman, good-looking as stink, with dark, curly hair and

a Ronald Colman mustache. What's more, he was the
salt of the bloody earth, a guy who would give you his
shirt, a swell pilot who flew alongside you as if he
were part of yourself. Before we had been sidekicking
a week Hether and I could go upstairs together like a
couple of dingbats and hit the ceiling way ahead of
any other twosome in Malta. Maybe Hether didn't
spend much time boning up on theory books, for the
guy was making a life study of draw poker. But what a
pilot! But about this scramble . . .

Our team was composed of Hether, McElroy,
Willie the Kid, Jonesy, Heslin, Al Yates, Chuck Ramsay, and myself. We got away in plenty of time and
bumped into the sweep at 26,000, where the Macchis
were flying. Hether started the show, as leader, by
diving through on the close escort. Seven Macchis
went down behind him. I slung into a dive behind
them, thinking Hether might be heading for trouble.
When I got there he seemed to be doing all right, so
I picked a Macchi for myself and we dogfought
awhile. The Eyetie went into a steep dive, pulled out
and twisted away, rolled and pulled up into a climb,
with Beurling chasing him. Finally he went into a
loop at the end of his climb and I nabbed him just at
its top. A two-second burst blew his cockpit apart.
The pilot baled in a hell of a hurry. I circled over him
as his parachute opened. He seemed to be healthy, so
I gave *May Day* on the RT, specifying that the gent

was an Italian, not one of our boys. That would give the ground his whereabouts and if the rescue launch wasn't too busy fishing our own fellows out of the sea they'd go and get him. I last saw him going into a cloud, downward bound.

McElroy got a Macchi on this scramble and Yates damaged an Me. The fellows from Luqa and Halfar had good hunting too, with the result that eight enemy aircraft were accounted for in less than an hour of battle, a total of seventeen enemy aircraft picked off in two scrambles. Our only loss, but a hard one to take, was Chuck Ramsay, as sober and conscientious a pilot as you could meet. Chuck simply disappeared from sight during the melee. Nobody saw what happened. When we all came home Chuck just wasn't there. Everybody had a pretty good idea that old Mother Mediterranean had claimed another good Canuck—so Chuck was chalked Missing.

The third scramble in which I had a share was a washout. Ops reported a big raid developing over Sicily and the Malta Spits were up in force to meet it. Jerry apparently thought better of the idea, because he didn't arrive in our neck of the woods. All in all, a good day. The boys had paid off, in part, for Smitty and Gil and Chuck!

Don't ever think poor old Malta wasn't taking one hell of a pasting, just because the Spits were up there giving the enemy a rubdown, however. Plenty of his raids were getting through and the island itself was pretty much of a shambles long before I ever saw it. At a rough guess three-quarters of the buildings in Valetta, the capital, were in ruins, and there were plenty of days when life was one constant alert. More than once a million pounds of concentrated muck have been dropped on the island in twenty-four hours. That's a lot of bombs on any target!

But the Malties were swell. Those guys really can take it. Everybody would stick right on the job until the last minute, diving for his own favorite glory hole only when he knew by the shriek of the bombs that this stick might be the one with his number on it. Malta, of course, probably has better air-raid shelters than any other place in the world, principally because it is just one huge rock. That kept the casualties down. The fact that there is practically no wood on the island, for the simple reason that no self-respecting tree can find a place for its roots, kept the fire hazard down. Buildings were knocked over like ninepins, but didn't burn. But there was more to it than that. What made the defense of Malta possible, the way I've always seen it, was the people. They were just plain, redheaded mad and their one-time pal, Mussolini, was one Grade A son of a bitch who'd stop at nothing, the double-crosser! That's the way the Malties saw it. Maybe the Jerries and the Eyeties might succeed in blowing them all into the Mediterranean, but nothing short of that would ever stop them, unless it was starvation. There was no fifth column on Malta in 1942, just 250,000 damned angry men, women, and kids.

At that you could have understood it if they'd been pretty well fed up with us, for don't ever think we had command of the air that summer. Sure, we were knocking down a damned sight more Jerries and Eyeties than they were getting Spits, but, hell, why wouldn't we? There were ten of them to every one on our side! We could harass them and we could shoot down a lot of them. But we couldn't stop those big jobs getting through and tossing down their tons of stuff every day—not so long as we had to worry about the gas ration, and the ack-ack gunners were limited to the number of rounds they could pour up at their guests.

The Malties, in other words, could take it—and they did. This was no Singapore. This was one tough island, inhabited by tough people. Not one of them had the slightest idea how long the grub would hold out. Not one knew when the Hun might try a landing. Lord knows he'd done his best to soften us up for it! But everybody on the island was hanging on by his teeth and the hell with the Huns and Mussolini. A great show!

On the 11th, Hether, Berkeley-Hill, Jonesy, and I were chased off the ground somewhere about nine

A.M. to meet nine Ju bombers and escort of approximately thirty assorted Me's, Macchis and Reggianes— the first time I had bumped into the last-named Italian species, a pretty good one. The raid swung in on Takali airdrome and wriggled in before we could get sufficient height to intercept. The Ju's dropped three or four delayed-action bombs on the west side of the field, wounding an erk, but doing no other damage. We didn't get near that mob . . . too late leaving the ground. The bombers got away clear, without a shot being fired. Half a dozen Macchis and a couple of the Reggianes dove through us as we climbed and sprayed us with lead as they passed and Jonesy picked up some bullet holes in his wings. Meanwhile Ops called through on the RT to tell us to keep on climbing, another raid was on the way. This time we were in better shape to meet 'em. Nine Ju's and an escort of more than forty fighters made up this show and the bombers actually got through over Takali, dropped their bombs—but missed the drome. We chased them thirty-five miles out to sea. There I got a chance to pick a Macchi from above. I went down vertically, about three hundred yards to his starboard side. He never saw me coming. At his own height, from an angle, I gave him a sharp one-second burst. The pilot baled out and one of the lads from a neighboring squadron saw him drifting down in his chute, confirming him as Destroyed.

Like almost every Malta air battle, the dog-
fighters had been split up, each man picking his own
opponent. Outnumbered, we were always the guys
behind the eight ball. So upstairs it was usually every
man for himself, every pilot's individual job to bore
in and try to break up the enemy's formation. Consequently, about half the time you didn't see what was
happening to your pals, because you were too busy
with your own job. If you spotted a guy in trouble
and could break loose from your own immediate en-
tanglements, you went to his aid. But most chaps who
went west during my months on Malta copped it when
they were alone and standing off three or four, or
even more, enemy aircraft. Nobody can ever say
enough about the guts, the individual he-man guts,
of that gang. They had plenty, and they needed 'em.

Berkeley-Hill got it just that way that morning.
When his string ran out B-H was attacking a decoy
Macchi and two Messerschmitts came out of the sun
at him, one from each side, and that was all. Just
before he went he had seen Hether pick off a Macchi
and confirmed it on the RT. "I saw it, Hether, old
boy!" were his words. Pretty sweet, when you think
of it, that a fellow's last, or next-to-last, act in this
world should be to confirm an enemy destroyed by
one of his pals. It hit Hether pretty hard, just the
same. For days the old chirp was gone, and not even
the dispersal poker game, which he loved next to fly-

ing, could lure him. We're a funny breed o' cats in this Spitfire business!

Jonesy bagged a Reggiane on the same scramble, a longish mix-up as these things go, lasting an hour and five minutes. Hether confirmed it for him. At least we had the consolation of a three-to-one score on the show.

Neither Hether nor I knew that Berkeley-Hill was down until we landed at Takali. We refueled at once and took off to search for him, hoping against hope to find him floating in his dinghy far out on the Mediterranean. After we had been searching about half an hour we ran into a couple of Macchis, looking for the lad I had shot down earlier. Low cloudbanks were moving in toward Malta and the Macchis were flying under them. We were out in the clear weather at the time. Hether immediately took height to go above the clouds and make sure nobody had a trap set for us. I gave chase to the Italians, one of whom was lagging behind the other. I picked the lagger, hoping to pot him before his mate knew I had joined the party. The boys must have been intent on the search for their missing sidekick, for I swear neither had seen me yet. I simply sneaked up behind the tail-ender and gave him a one-second squirt. He burst into flames and went down. Without further ado I whipped around on the other lad and gave him the old one-two. He dived-in beside his mate. From the firing of the first shot until both Macchis went down no more than six or seven seconds had elapsed. Things happen fast in this racket.

Right then Hether appeared, diving through the clouds to look for me. We were too low to talk on RT, but I waggled my wings and beckoned and he came along over the spot where the two Eyeties had gone in. What had happened was plain as your nose to see. In any event the radio plot at Ops clearly showed what had happened, for at 10:41 four aircraft were shown in the area twenty miles northeast of Zonkor Point, at which moment the number faded to two, Hether and myself. We took part in a third scramble later in the day, but nothing came of it. Three to show for the day's work!

The 13th was quiet, the 14th unlucky for me, but a good day for everybody else. We had only one scramble against a flock of Schmitts and Macchis. I was chased up high, alone, to hunt high fliers, the sweep itself coming in low. Upstairs I spotted a batch of Macchis, traveling in a tight V about five hundred feet below me and a mile away. I went in to break them up. As I did, three Messerschmitts and two Reggianes came out of the sun at me from opposite angles, putting the scissors on me. I had to break one way or the other in a hurry, so I decided to let the Reggianes shoot at me, as they have less fire power than Me's. The bastards riddled the old Spit! They put better than twenty bullets through the fuselage and wings. An explosive bullet nicked my right heel. I did a half-roll and went away in a hurry as another bunch of Reggianes ganged me. From that moment the Spit was in no shape to fight, but I messed around and kept our friends as busy as I could, keeping clear of any close-in action. That was another time young Beurling hadn't kept his eyes peeled! Apart from my troubles, it was a good show. Eight Huns and Eyeties went into the drink in all. Hether nabbed one and Willie the Kid another, the only hits scored by 249. I limped home to be kidded to death by the rest of the guys for getting myself shot up. "Now maybe you'll learn to keep your tail clean, Beurling," was the Kid's salutation. I had it coming. The doctor fished bits of bullet out of my heel and told me to take the rest of the day off.

Nothing but a routine patrol on the 15th. That night Wing Commander Gracey came around to the mess. "Sergeant Beurling," he said, grinning and looking fussed, "I have the honor to inform you that his Majesty has graciously consented . . ." What he meant was that I'd won the D.F.M.

(ROBERTS: The young man said he hadn't the slightest idea what had been said in the citation for his Distinguished Flying Medal. As a matter of fact, he said, he couldn't recall ever having seen it. "You know how those things go," he said. "Just a lot of words." Did he mean, I

asked, that decorations and suchlike are things he doesn't
set much store by: that he didn't give a hoot, for example,
whether he had a D.F.M. or not? "God, no!" he answered,
sitting bolt upright in bed. "That is the one gong that
means something. You know what it means? It means all
the time I spent trying to earn money for flying time to
get a license. It means that trip across Canada on the rods
and the Seattle hoosegow and the long trek back. It means
my attempts to get into the Canadian, Chinese, and Finnish Air Forces and three trips across the Atlantic in a
munitions ship to get into the RAF. It means all the
months of training in England and the hell of a time I
had to get posted to a front where I could get some fighting
and prove to everybody else what I had known for years
about myself. Yes, sir. That's the real one, that D.F.M.
That's the one I treasure more than all the others. I
figure I won that one the hard way. The others came along
in 'due course!' "

I dug up the citation and took it along to show the
hero. It said: "Sergeant Beurling has displayed great skill
and courage in the face of the enemy." It described en-
gagements recorded in earlier paragraphs, up to July 6th,
at which time he had destroyed five enemy aircraft and
damaged three others over Occupied France and at Malta.
The young man read the document and grinned. "Lots
of two-dollar words, huh?" was his comment.)

A two weeks' lull hit us about this time, during
which I participated in three scrambles, only one of
which developed into anything resembling a major
fracas. But we knew the Big Show wasn't over, for
Intelligence reported steady activity over Sicily way.

The breathing space was not without its tragedy,
however, for on the 19th Jean Paradis was shot down,

during a show when the luck ran against us. Only two of our Spits were engaged, Jean and a newcomer, the rest being from Halfar and Luqa. Trouble was the boys couldn't find the bombers and had split to go hunting around. Jean found them first. His last call: "I see the bom-bairs. I go there!" gave their location to Ops, but by the time the others reached the spot Jean was gone.

Although I was never much of a fellow to form close friendships, Jean and I had always been good pals. Only a couple of days before his last scramble we had gone swimming together at Siliema and sat around on the white rocks talking about home and what we were going to do when the shooting stopped. Would a guy stay in the Air Force if he could? Would he go looking for somebody else's war, or become an international flying policeman, if that's the way they sugar it off? Would he go into commercial aviation, or try to start a show of his own, or what? One thing was sure, we agreed. It had to be some kind of flying. What else is there? We had talked like that awhile, then flopped off the rocks like a couple of seals into the green water, so clear that you could swim around with your eyes open and watch the fish go by. The war had been a hell of a long way off, that afternoon.

But there was more to our talk than shop. When we got off alone Jean and I were just a couple of kids who lived within a hundred miles of each other back home, halfway across the world. You could say: "Remember the Malteds you could get at the soda bar on such-and-such a Montreal corner?" That would start a whole hour of reminiscence, for Jean could never talk enough about Canada and his beloved Province of Quebec. With most of the fellows, no matter how friendly we had become, no matter how much we had flown together, I didn't seem to have much supply of conversation. They had wives, or girls, or pet hobbies, or the stud game, to talk about and wrangle over. I seemed to be bothered with a one-track mind. Once I got through with shop talk, or with kidding around a bit, I ran out of things to discuss. But I could always get back home in a talk with Jean, out on the Siliema rocks. He might be putting in time on a barren island in the middle of the Mediterranean, but his heart was still back in his Laurentian Hills, around Shawinigan. Oh, well . . .

The day Berkeley-Hill went west a new gang of Spits and pilots had flown in from a carrier and were getting acclimatized during the lull. One of their number had gone into the sea getting off the flight deck, but the others had come through without incident. The lads who came to 249 were preponderantly North American, five Canucks and three Yanks out of a total of eleven new pilots. The Canadians were Junior Moody, Red Bryden, Stan ("Scarlet") Shewell of Owen Sound, Ontario (who always claimed he was a natural for a V.C., since Billy Bishop had started from the same place!), Hogy Hogarth, and Pete Carter, a Westerner. Junior was the only guy with commissioned rank—a "Prog PO" by RAF definition, but don't ask me what *Prog* means; I wouldn't know. The Yanks were Smoky Joe Lowry, undisputed crap-shooting champion of Malta, Pete Peters of Texas, who had flown for the Spanish Loyalists, and Georgia Wynn, with whom I was to do God knows how many scrambles in the days ahead. Smoky Joe was a prog, the others were sergeants. Giddy Giddings and Gass were England's contribution, Hiskens was Australia's. Mostly they were a gang of laughing guys.

Changes had taken place in the direction of Takali. Everybody had felt like hell to see Wing Commander Gracey go back to England on rest. He'd been Mr. Malta and the dump wouldn't be like home without him. But our former squadron leader, Grant, upped to wingco and commanding the Takali station, was a right guy and Mitch Mitchell who came over from our companion squadron to take over 249 was another. So we were still okay.

Of the gang who had been on deck when I arrived only Willie the Kid, Jonesy, Micky Butler, Jack Rae, Mac MacLean, Bob Middlemiss and Al Yates remained. Of the June arrivals McElroy, Lattimer, de l'Ara, Rip Mutch, Baxter, Budd, and myself were still going strong. Smitty, Kelly, Ramsay, Gilbert,

Tommy Tompkins, Berkeley-Hill, and Jean Paradis had all been knocked out of the play by the Hun. Daddy Longlegs, Norm Lee, de Nencrede, Brennan, and Heslin had gone back to England for rest and furlough. That's the way it seems to add up, looking back from here. But faces and names change so quickly in spots like Malta that it is impossible to check off the list of who was with you at such-and-such a day. All you can remember sharply is the things you did with those who were your day-by-day scramble mates. But back to the lull . . .

Hether, Willie, Micky Butler, and I scrambled together on the 18th, but by the time we were up high the show was over. On the 19th I went up for the tail end of the raid on which Paradis was shot down and flew again later to meet a fighter sweep which didn't materialize. The 20th was a washout. The 21st featured a washout patrol and the 22nd was another blank. That was okay by us. The Malta gas ration wouldn't be so hot until another convoy came through from Gib. Then the balloon went up again!

The scene in dispersal when the call "Scramble Tiger Squadron!" came through during the morning of the 23rd was something for the movies. In the center of the hut a hot stud game was in progress. Tables, cards, and everybody's bankroll hit the floor as Hether, Shewell, the Kid, Bryden, Giddy, Georgia, and Hogarth swarmed for the door. Rae baled out the window behind me. Squadron Leader Mitchell was somewhere in the melee. Hether, Georgia, Willie, and I were the first four off. As we pulled up our undercarts and began to climb, Ops called "Gain angels quickly!" and we hit 22,000 before you could say "wink." As we did, three Ju's and about forty fighters hove in sight at about 15,000 and we went to work. From the sun a cloud of Spits went down through the top-cover fighters to get at the bombers. Mitchell knocked one off as we went through, his Jerry hitting the sea in a cloud of smoke from its engines. I damaged another, catching him in the 88's weak spot, the starboard engine, without which he can't maintain height and to which the whole hydraulic system, controlling his undercarriage, is hitched. Hit an 88 in the starboard engine and you have a Jerry as good as Destroyed, even though he may manage to limp home. Hether damaged the third bomber and had his starboard engine smoking as he broke for Sicily. I'll take a bet those Junkers' crews were gray-headed by the time they crash-landed at home. We sure had put on a party for them!

The fighters came diving down after us as we went for the bombers. A Reggiane and I chased each other around for a hell of a time, looping, rolling, doing tight turns, diving on and away from each other and generally helling around the sky. At last I managed to get in a quarter-attack from below, behind, and to port. It was a pure deflection shot and it blew his left wing off. He fell over, streaming smoke, and plowed into the sea. None of his pals came to his aid, but left us to dogfight it out.

Red Bryden made his first kill on this party, dropping an Me with a quick burst. Rae bagged another. We all got home. Three washout days followed.

The 27th was my biggest day on Malta. At six A.M. Bryden, Willie, Georgia, Scarlet, Micky Butler, Hogarth, Hether, and I scrambled to intercept a fifty-plus attack from seven Ju 88s and their fighter escort. We slammed up the hill to 25,000, where the fighters were covering the bombers. The Ju's were just going to work on Takali when we came along and they plastered the joint, leaving the drome pocked with bomb craters. I was the lucky lad who spotted the sweep and called into the RT: "Enemy aircraft at four o'clock, slightly below!" and led the gang in, with everybody hotfooting after me. I spotted four Machis running in line astern and took Number Four. They saw me coming and pulled into a climbing turn to the right. As they did I came up on my man's starboard quarter and let him have a burst. It was a straight deflection shot which went into his engine and radiator. He flicked into a spin, but managed to pull out and crash-landed on Gozo, able to walk away from the mess.

A second or so later I got Number Three exactly

the same way. The poor devil simply blew to pieces in the air.

Just as I was about to turn my attention to Number Two I spotted a couple of Messerschmitts directly under me, so instead of pressing the attack on the Macchis, I half-rolled and shot down past the Me's, pulling up sharply under their bellies. I let the first guy have it full-out and caught him in the gas tank. Down he went. I still had time for a shot at his teammate and blew pieces off his wings and tail. He flew off in a hurry, skidding all over the sky. What happened to him God knows.

It had been a pretty good party. Bryden shot down his second Schmitt and must have killed the pilot, for the ship dived straight into the sea from 20,000 feet. Willie the Kid picked off another with a pretty deflection shot. Hether damaged another.

As we disentangled ourselves and started for home, Ops ordered us to keep the hell away from Takali, as the Ju's had wrecked the place. We dropped into Luqa instead and had scarcely refueled and refilled our magazines before another scramble call came through and Hether, Willie, Bryden, and I were off to the races again. This time four 88s came over, escorted by about twenty Messerschmitts and we came in for the second act. The Luqa and Halfar lads had gone up first and destroyed all four bombers before they even reached the Maltese coast. As we climbed, the sky was white with parachuting Germans from the big jobs, the Me's circling around to protect the riders from harm. We got above the Me's at 17,000. To start the doings Willie and Red went down through the Messerschmitts, five of which promptly jumped on Willie and shot his Spitter full of daylight. I horned in and followed the Me's down. Three promptly went away from there, but two stayed to fight. I started chasing one of them around in tight turns and we split-assed uphill and downdale until he went into a dive to get away. I went along, picked him up in the sights and put a one-second squirt into his glycol tank. He rolled over and went into the sea from 1,000 feet. During this mix-up I had been on the second Me's tail for a split-second, just long enough to give him a quick one. He streamed black, oily smoke from his engine and was last seen by Hether, running for cover. Whether he reached Sicily or not, I have no idea. He was counted Damaged.

Flying a Spitter full of holes apparently meant nothing to our lighthearted Willie. Deciding it would be safer on the ground than riding around in a sieve, the Kid had pulled out of the mix-up and put his nose down for Luqa. On the way down, however, he spotted an Me all by its lonesome. Cold meat, Willie decided, going into his dive. He was right. One quick squirt and Jerry burst into flames and went into the sea. This time Willie didn't hover around to watch him go.

"You know, George," the Kid said, as we were lolling around in the mess that night, "there's no trick to potting Jerries if you keep your wits about you. The blighters almost ask you to shoot them down!"

"Sure," I said, "but did you ever hear what happens to boys whose tails get dirty?"

"Aw, nuts, big shot," Willie grinned. "Listen to the guy who shoots down his daily dozen! . . . Listen, hermit! What say we go places tonight?"

That was one night I'd have been ready for anything. Instead, I had a date to keep with Intelligence, to visit the Eyetie who had crashed on Gozo. The gent was a flight sergeant by the name of Cino Valentini who had been in the Air Force since 1936 and the last five months in Sicily, during which time he had shot down three Spitfires. He and I didn't make much progress toward world peace, I'm afraid. He asked me what I thought of Italian pilots and I said: "You're pretty good, but your tactics stink." He asked what I meant by that and I replied: "Well, for one thing, your formations are too tight. You have to spend so damned much time concentrating on the formation, keeping out of the other guys' slipstreams and away from wingtips that you don't get a chance to look around." Valentini said that's the way they teach it in the Italian Air Force, as if that made it right. I gathered he didn't think I knew what I was talking about. To him I was just a stiff who had been lucky enough to shoot down a real pilot. I suppose he figured that if any of us had any brains we wouldn't have been hanging around Malta. Well, who was bragging about brains? Not the Spitfire guys, that's sure. The Intelligence bloke and the Eyetie jabbered in Italian awhile. Then Intelligence explained they were discussing when and how the war would end.

"Our friend here is convinced his side can't lose," he grinned. "Anything you'd like to ask about that, sergeant?"

"Ask him," I answered, "why, if that's so, Italian pilots have baled over Malta without anybody firing a shot at them, carrying their toothbrushes and shaving kit? Ask him if he remembered to bring his pajamas."

Probably *I'd* be a cocky bird if ever I had to bale over Sicily and the Macaronis asked me the score. But somehow I didn't cotton to Signor Valentini. He sure thought Old Muss-face had done plenty for Italy. Wonder how he feels since Montgomery rolled up through Libya!

The next day things were quiet, so Rae and I hoicked over to Siliema to swim. Jerry behaved like a gentleman all afternoon and you wouldn't have dreamed a war was going on within a million miles, certainly not that you were living on an island in a state of siege, as you stretched out on the rocks and soaked up sun. According to the Germans, we were "the 250,000 prisoners of Malta." That was the phrase their radio always used when they were blitzing us from the air, trying to kid the Malties into quitting, or slitting our throats, or something. They didn't know the Maltese very well, I guess. Sure, they were prisoners who had been told by Lord Gort, when he arrived to take charge of the siege, that everybody better pull in his belt, because we were all going to tough it out together, even Stephen. Did that worry the Maltese? Not much! Too bad Jerry never could see the way they would gather around the headlands and yell "Hooray!" every time another Me hit the deck. Great guys! They sure earned that medal Churchill sent them!

Apparently the big schemozzle of the 27th had taken a lot of steam out of the Sicily boys. No wonder. They'd lost a flock of bombers and fighters on the busy day. You could almost feel the heat dying down in the days that followed. The feeling was in the air that Malta had won another round. That didn't please me too well. I'd come far enough to realize I had Jerry's number, provided I kept my own eyes peeled. That's a good feeling, and when you have it you don't like to taper off. I'd put in too many months before coming to Malta, flying now and then and getting little action. The idea of loafing around dispersal for days on end without getting off the ground, with nothing to do but slug through textbooks, or try to work out new shooting theories on paper, didn't appeal to me as the best way of putting in days, or weeks, waiting for Jerry to heal his wounds and begin again. I could do my paper work after dark! But the choice between tapering off or scrambling didn't rest with us. In any case, there was no denying the fact that our Spits would be better for a little more attention than our overworked erks had been able to give them the last few weeks. Certainly fuel conservation was greatly to be desired until the next convoy arrived to replenish Malta's storage tanks. No wonder the Hun runs second in so many wars!

The finale of the Big Blitz came on the 29th. In it Jerry covered himself with no glory at all. He started the day by coming halfway across from Sicily in force—and turning back. An hour or so later Hether and Scarlet came tearing out of the stud game, Ernie Budd from a good book, and I from a kibitzer's seat to intercept a sweep of twenty Messerschmitts at 28,000 feet. That gave Jerry five-to-one odds, which isn't bad in any race. Under those conditions you would think he'd stay and fight until he had you all down in the sea or had to leg for home for more gas. Not Jerry. Always a great guy for his plate of cold meat, Jerry, but not one with a liking for a cut off the hot roast!

Hether and Budd promptly tangled with five of

the Messerschmitts and Scarlet and I found ourselves milling around in the middle of a mess of fifteen Germans, dogfighting all over the ruddy sky. In twos and threes they started to break off, suddenly remembering important dates back in Sicily, no doubt. You almost had to act like a decoy duck to get anybody to come in and fight, but at last one of the gang decided I was all set up for him. I nearly was, at that. Out of the sun he came in a hurry, giving me a burst from the port quarter which shot the hood off my cockpit. As he went past I laced into him. By the time I got my sights on him we must have been 450 yards apart, but I gave him a one-second burst which got him in the engine, the gas tank, and the cockpit. He went down in flames and crashed into the sea about a mile off Valetta. Budd blew the tail off another, which also plunged into the drink. That was the end of the big July Blitz.

As we turned our noses towards Takali I heard voices on the RT.

"What'd you have in that last hand, Scarlet?"

"Aces back to back, dammit," the answer came back. "I'll bet those goddam burglars stole my pot!"

(ROBERTS: Young Beurling had proved his point. He had established as fact the assumption that he could shoot down enemy aircraft by destroying fifteen, damaging five, and probably destroying another between the 6th and the 29th of July. Actually the job had been done in seven flying days. Jerry had bumped head-on into a perfectionist, a kid who lived for the job of flying. The July Blitz had done something for its hero too. It had made a real team player out of a youngster who had specialized in individualism in such degree in the beginning that his value to the team had sometimes been questioned. But wise men like Gracey and Grant and Laddie Lucas had seen something pretty special in their young individualist. They gave him his head and at the same time taught him to play for the team. Somewhere there is the secret of what happened at Malta in July of '42. The kid was happy and at ease for the first time since the war began. He didn't play poker. He didn't take a drink. He'd rather fly hungry than on a full stomach, because he believed hunger sharpened his eyesight. His flying mates had come to rely on him as the fellow who could always spot the enemy before the Huns saw the Spitfires. His marksmanship was nothing short of miraculous. Every one of his bag had been shot down by a single burst from his Spitfire's guns, often by a staccato one-second squirt. Virtually every enemy aircraft had been the victim of pure deflection shooting. A lone hunter by instinct, he had nevertheless become one of the 249 team—its unofficial field captain.

The last man on earth to support the assumption that he had won the July Blitz singlehanded would be George Beurling. He hadn't. It was won by the team, by the lads of Luqa and Halfar and the "guys" from Takali. On the altar of war had gone Smitty and Gilbert, Chuck Ramsay, Berkeley-Hill and Jean Paradis, before them Kelly and Tommy Tompkins. But 249 had avenged them by destroying nine or ten Messerschmitts, Macchis, Reggaines or Ju 88s for every Malta Spitter to go down.

As the July Blitz ended, new honors came to George Beurling. Promotion from sergeant to pilot officer (the

RAF's equivalent of second lieutenant) came on July 30th. This time no questions were asked, no opportunity given to sidestep by saying: "I'd rather stay in the ranks, if it's all the same to you, sir!" Gracey, Grant, and Lucas had seen to that. The record has it that the young man moved his gear over to the officers' quarters, then went roaming in his Spitfire "to see if I felt any different"! . . . "Hell," he says, "you wore the same clothes. All you do is take down your stripes and put up officer's insignia. The grub isn't a damn bit better and you catch the Malta Dog just as easily! Anyway, everybody looks alike to Jerry or floating around the sea in a Mae West!"

That was not all. Although the citation did not come through from Middle East Headquarters for another month, it was for his great work in July that Beurling was given a Bar to his Distinguished Flying Medal. The "papers" specifically mentioned his destruction of four enemy aircraft in one day and added: "His courage and determination are a source of inspiration to all.")

CHAPTER VII

Malta Hangs On

THERE is a tendency to talk about the weeks which followed the July Blitz as if they were a period of peace and quiet. "This," you start out to say, "was the real Big Lull. Nothing happened."

Then you thumb through the record and you recall what a hell of a time the convoy had getting into port with food for half-starved Malta. You turn the page and remember the big day when the gang shot up the enemy's airfield over on Sicily and the thrill everybody got out of pasting Jerry for a change. Then there was the day the Jerries shot you down and had you wondering if they could use any mouth-organ players Up Yonder to help the harpists out. . . . So this was the Big Lull. Nothing ever happened!

I celebrated the coming of the Lull by picking up my first good dose of the Dog. From the 2nd to the 7th of August the ghost of George Beurling hung around the pilots' quarters, afraid to venture out in public for the first couple of days, then too weak to go out, even if he'd had the ambition. "That's what you get for eating your spinach!" the veterans of other Bitch Blitzes would rib. "You'll never be the same again!" They were right. For the rest of my days on Malta, like pretty nearly everybody else, I lived in a state of unpleasant uncertainty. The Dog was Jerry's secret weapon of siege, and I don't mean maybe!

By the 8th I was around again, feeling pretty wispy, but bound I'd fly, as about half of 249 was Dog-ridden by then. That was the day I took my first good peek through the Pearly Gates.

It happened soon after ten in the morning. Jonesy, Georgia Wynn, Ernie Budd, and I were chased upstairs to meet an incoming raid, but when we reached 20,000 feet and were cruising around we couldn't see a sign of the enemy. Budd had turned back with engine trouble and Jonesy, who was leading, called back to Ops to ask: "Anything doing up here, or not?" After a moment's silence Ops replied: "Party of fifteen plus, about twenty miles north of your position, coming south. Gain more angels!" Right then we spotted them and they spotted us; a whole slew of fighters, sitting right above us. "Up we go!" Jonesy yelled into the mike—and up we went!

Fifteen yellow-nosed Me 109s were waiting for us and every mother's son of 'em stayed to fight. Why wouldn't they, at odds of five-to-one and the favorites up high, running in the rail position? We split up and bored in and I got in a burst at one bird, who promptly pulled up sharp, dived, and headed off toward Sicily. Right then three Huns leaped out of the sun at *me*. I turned quickly to get under one of them and gave him a two-and-a-half second burst with everything I had, just as I rolled over to dive. My burst got him in the glycol tank and the engine and he didn't even stop to catch his breath, but plunged straight for the sea, where Jonesy saw him hit the deck. Almost in the same instant Jonesy got a Jerry too, which I confirmed. Georgia shot another full of holes and scored a Damaged. My guy, by the way, was a full deflection shot.

I hadn't any more than begun to dive when I got mine—a couple of bullets right in the engine. The throttle wouldn't grab hold and after a minute or so the engine decided it would like to call it a day and seize-up. There was I, spang in the middle of a skyful of Jerries and my motive power gone lame!

A couple of Huns were perched above me, slightly off to one side, but didn't see me, thank God, or I'd have been cold turkey for them. I didn't dare call Jonesy on the RT and tell him my plight, or he'd have quit the dogfight of which he was the center of attraction and come hurrying over to help me—bringing all his friends with him, no doubt. Over to the north I could see Georgia split-assing all over heaven, entertaining four or five Jerries. No use calling him, either. So I decided to quietly get the hell out of there—if I could.

The old Merlin wouldn't give me any more than 160 miles an hour and was heating up fast. The Spit was sinking slowly. It began to look like a baling job. Thank God, the Huns didn't seem to have registered

my departure! By the time I reached the Maltese coast I was down to 2,000 feet and doubting strongly my ability to get home. I prepared to bale. That's what orders tell you to do, if in trouble below 3,000 feet and not over an airdrome. Then I made the discovery that my parachute straps were pretty loose and said to myself: "If you ever try jumping into that rig, you're going to rupture yourself when the umbrella opens,

my friend!" Before that I'd undone my Sutton
harness, to free myself from the cockpit, and by the
time I'd snapped it on again, so as not to fall forward
in a crash landing, I'd lost another big piece of height
and was skipping cross-country about 200 feet above
the ground. By this time the engine was finished and
the prop dead. Right ahead I could see a nice, plowed
field, about an acre in size, surrounded by low stone
walls. If I could sneak into that, I'd be okay.

I skithered along, cutting the glide fine, but not
too fine. It's damned easy to flick these Spits and spin
in when you try keeping that nose high. As I came
close in over the near wall I put the left wing down
to take up the bump and bellied down onto the
ground. The wing absorbed the wallop and stopped
me cold, which was okay by me. The far wall was too
near for comfort. I climbed out, unhurt excepting a
superficial cut in one arm, and looked the ship over.
She had taken little damage, excepting those bullets
in the engine.

From the field I made my way to the main road
and sat down on a wall to wait for somebody to come
along. The first vehicle to appear was a military truck.
I thumbed the driver, who took me all the way to
Takali, where the gang were counting me a goner.
Both Georgia and Jonesy had been so damned busy
keeping open house for Jerry when I left that they
figured I must have been shot down into the sea dur-

ing the brawl. Hether looked up from the hand he was betting and said: "He deserves all he gets, for leaving his luck at home!" The old Flying Yorkshireman, God bless him!

The 9th and 10th were quiet, which was fine by me, because I was feeling like the concentrated wrath of God. On the 9th I was up for the better part of an hour, on what turned out to be a pure routine affair, as no Jerries arrived. That evening Hether and I flipped over to Sicily, looking for an alleged E-boat pack, the Germans' torpedo-carrying motor launches. We saw none. Never have seen any, as a matter of fact. We didn't see any Jerries either, nor get ourselves ack-acked, although we flew in and out the bays no more than ten or twelve feet above the beach. We hung around Sicily for about twenty-five minutes, then went home.

I crawled around like a wraith all day on the 10th and didn't leave the ground. The 11th found me back in quarters, a prisoner of the Dog again. That was the day of the big convoy show, and I had to miss it!

Most of us on Malta hadn't known how fine the mixture was cut, those days. I don't suppose the ordinary guy in Leningrad ever really stopped to add up the score either. All you could do was keep plugging. There was always talk flying around about shortages of this-and-that and it was common gossip that the

Higher Command had established a Target Day that was sort of the island's aim. That, summed up, meant neither more nor less than keeping going until there was nothing left to keep going on. If we'd stopped to think, we'd have realized we must be pretty short of fuel to keep the Spitters flying, because we sure hadn't been scrambling any clouds of fighters the last little while.

Over in London they knew all about our plight and they'd decided to shove the biggest convoy through to Malta they'd ever attempted. As we heard it, fourteen merchantmen and tankers made up the original party and at Gib they were given the biggest protecting screen the navy could dig up, including an aircraft carrier, complete with fighters. Apparently everything went along pretty well until the convoy approached the narrow straits between Cape Bon, at the tip of Tunisia, and the western end of Sicily. Then the Germans started to paste it to them with submarines and surface craft (it was their nest Hether and I'd been looking for the day before, only we hadn't known the purpose of the trip). Ju 88s and Cants blasted the ships with bombs and particular hell was raised all over the sea. It must have been a flaming show, while it lasted.

Our guys didn't get into the earlier part of the mill, which was beyond our effective range. But they were called out as the battle came nearer home and they tussled it out with the Jerries and the Eyeties while the remaining merchantmen, by now scattered from convoy formation, limped into Valetta's Grand Harbour, one by one. Six ships got through—not a tanker among them!

That was the 11th. That day and the 12th I lay around quarters, completely be-Dogged and damning the luck. On the 13th, however, I managed to crawl down to the drome and went out with Jonesy, Scarlet, and Georgia to fly ahead of the cruisers and destroyers which had come in with the convoy and were about to hotfoot back to Gib. Their aircraft carrier, of course, hadn't come all the way in with them. Whether it had turned back to Gibraltar or was waiting for them up west, I don't know. All I know is what *our* job was. That's all you ever get to know anyway— and usually that's enough.

Apparently the Huns didn't expect the navy to leave just yet, because the sneak play worked fine. We were looking for bombers and fighters in droves, but all the time we were out we encountered just one lone Ju 88. Believe me, he got little chance to phone home and tell the folks what was going on!

Early in the expedition Shewell had to leave us and go back with engine trouble. That left three of us and we mucked along at about 10,000 feet until we were eighty or ninety miles west of Malta. Out there we decided to go higher and skithered up to 18,000.

I YELLED INTO THE MIKE, "LOOK OUT! HERE I COME!" AND
WHIZZED DOWN

That's where we found our lonely Ju, cruising around all by himself.

Jonesy called through: "Here's where I get some head-on practice!" and slammed into the Jerry, rolling over and diving away, just as he let go his burst. I went up above, drawing back as I climbed and circling over to starboard, my favorite spot. That put me about 2,000 feet above the Jerry, to starboard and behind. As I got ready to go down on him I heard Georgia's voice call: "Don't shoot the bastard down all by your-self, Jonesy! Let me have a pot at him too!" Then I saw Georgia go in head-on and pull up over the bomber, which just kept plowing along, straight ahead, the best thing it could do under the circum-stances. I yelled into the mike: "Look out! Here I come!" and whizzed down, putting a two-second burst into the starboard engine as I went past. The engine fell off. The bomber burst into flames and down it went. Not one of its four-man crew got a chance to bale. We sure had let daylight into the Ju! Georgia's attack had put cannon shells into the fuselage and Jonesy had peppered the nose and wings. I'd nabbed his weak spot, the starboard engine. It was the first, and last, setup I ever saw at Malta. The Hun certainly wasn't out navy-hunting. They'd never send one lone-some bomber for a job like that! Must have been a reconnaissance of some kind, maybe trying to find out if any odds and ends of the convoy were still drifting around the sea, waiting for a kindly Hun to knock them off. Whatever it was, that was one German bomber crew whose luck was out that day. We scored one-third apiece for the job.

Next day we flew over the merchantmen in Valetta harbor, where the RAF was maintaining constant protective patrols. Jerry, strange to say, wasn't making much trouble. We were helped by low-lying clouds and knew from Ops that the enemy bombers were coming to the edge of the cloud layer, just two or three miles offshore. Over the harbor we had a high, clear ceiling and I guess the Huns wouldn't risk sticking their noses out, figuring we'd probably drop on them and gang 'em if they ever came into the clear. If they'd only known our strength! Most of the time I provided the "screen" I was all alone, my only partner having gone back with engine trouble soon after we began our patrol and nobody coming up to take his place.

Next day we went out to meet a torpedoed tanker and once again I sat around marveling at the guts of the guys who go to sea. This time, however, I felt safer than on the occasions when I'd been on shipboard, wondering who'd hit us with what. This time I was riding in my own element, the air.

She was the U.S. tanker *Ohio* and when they'd caught her, out west of Sicily, they'd blasted the hell out of her from the air, then plunked a torpedo into her belly for luck, and left her to sink. She'd lost her escort. She'd lost the convoy. The poor devil was in a hell of a mess, but still trying to plug through with that load of gas which might save Malta for the United Nations. When first the skipper broke radio silence it was to say that he was coming along, making about three knots. Then Malta heard that he was being socked again by Ju's and another message came through to say that the tanker was drifting around and that the master didn't even know his position. Right then somebody thought of the navy—or maybe the navy was actually going out to look for him the day we shot down the lonely Ju, though I don't think so—and a couple of the destroyers picked the *Ohio* up, just about the time the skipper was deciding to abandon ship. When we came along, damned if they hadn't lashed the poor old tanker between the two warships and were limping together into port. And they made it!

All Malta was out on the headlands to see the strange trio make harbor. It was sort of a triumphal procession, with Spitfires split-assing overhead and crowds cheering and all hell let generally loose. That tanker's arrival meant plenty to Hitler's so-called "250,000 prisoners." It meant, for one thing, that Target Day was pushed ahead. Malta was still in there punching. So the old *Ohio* wallowed in, and when they unhitched her from the destroyers she just settled on the harbor bottom, like the tuckered old girl she was, barely high enough out of water to get the pumps working on her load of precious aviation spirit.

That flip over the tanker was Bob Seed's first patrol over Malta, where he'd arrived just a couple of days before with a new batch of pilots from Gib and had been posted to 249. Were we ever glad to see each other! And did I watch Bob's tail like a mother hen, even though we weren't bothered by Huns. Force of habit, I guess. 249 had a new CO too. Squadron Leader Wood, who, like every Wood I ever met in the RAF, promptly became *Timber* to all his associates. He had been in 72 Squadron with Jonesy in Britain and had won the D.F.C., to which he added a Bar in Malta. Timber had spent the better part of his life in British Columbia as a transplanted Englishman and was one swell guy. Group Captain Churchill, D.S.O., D.F.C., was another newcomer with Bob's gang and became our station commander at Takali. A very keen CO, with seven or eight Jerries to his credit from the Battle of Britain. Wing Commander Donaldson arrived about this time, with the same gang, I guess, and Johnnie Farmer, Stead, and Sandy Sanderson joined 249 as pilots. The rest of the new bunch went to other squadrons on the island.

Right through this period I was struggling with the Dog, and not making much headway with the struggle. Once up in the air I'd feel all right, and sucking in oxygen would give me a temporary pickup. But as soon as I was back on the ground I'd be weaving again, from plain, everyday weakness. I spent the 16th and 17th back in quarters, but got back to duty on the 18th in time to help turn back a fighter sweep of Macchis, Reggianes, and Me's, about sixteen strong, who were probably feeling inquisitive about the merchantmen still riding in the harbor. They didn't get near them, but they did shoot down one of our best guys, Mac MacLean.

Eight of us scrambled to meet the sweep: Squadron Leader Mitchell, MacLean, Hether, Micky Butler, Bryden, Georgia, Scarlet Shewell, and myself. As we were climbing, trying to get over the visitors, a couple of the Reggianes dived and caught Mac offguard, smack in the engine. He took fire and was trapped in his burning Spitter for a full minute while Bryden, who had pulled out of formation, circled him, hoping. God! It must have been a hotbox, that cockpit! Mac was so badly singed he could barely use his right hand to get rid of his Sutton harness. There he was, right in the middle of a burning barn, trying to wriggle loose and get over on his back. Red said later: "I damn near burst into tears for joy, when I saw the Spitter roll over and Mac fall out!" But Mac was still having hand trouble and couldn't even yank his ripcord. Bryden told us the poor devil must have fallen 6,000 feet before the chute opened. Then Bryden *May-Dayed* and came on up to join the rest of us.

Mac landed in the sea and managed to get rid of his parachute, but was so weak and so badly burned he couldn't get his dinghy out. He floated around about four miles off the coast for fifteen minutes in his Mae West, until the rescue launch came out and got him. Burns all over his arms, chest and face, and around his thighs and groin, were just about enough to kill the poor devil, but he pulled through. He lay abed in Malta's hospital for a month, too weak to be moved. Then he was flown to Gibralter and on to England where, the last I heard, he was recuperating. Mac had gone through a long pull on Malta and was just about ready for a rest—but what a hell of an experience to have to go through to get it.

On the 19th a sudden cloudburst washed the Takali field right out of the picture, just as if they'd lifted the Mediterranean up and dropped it on us. The next day, for the first time since my coming to Malta, the RAF's Spitfires went on the offensive— and couldn't even get a Hun or a Eyetie to come up and argue with them over the enemy's home grounds.

Two full squadrons participated. We formed up south of the island and whisked across the water in three layers, eight aircraft at 27,000 feet, eight at 28,500, and eight at 30,000. I flew with the middle eight. We swept into Sicily over Cape Scaramia and

took a look at each of the main enemy fields at Comiso,
Biscari, and Gela. Not a Jerry stirred. Not a drop of
flak was poured up at us. We rolled along, coming out
over Cape Scaramia and beetled home. Nothing much
to it, bar the pleasure of sticking your nose into the
enemy's country for a change.

We tried it again three days later, after our ships
had been laid up for a check-over. But once again the
enemy refused to play, though a few fighters were
sitting around, away up high. Group Captain
Churchill led the show, followed by Wing Commander Donaldson, who had taken over from Grant
at Takali, and Squadron Leader Wood, 249's new
skipper, relieving Mitchell, who'd gone back to England. Hether, Willie the Kid, Scarlet Shewell, Georgia,
and I made up the rest of the team. We came over
Sicily at 18,000 and were just beginning to hunt
around when the wingco developed air-screw trouble.
So we cut the sweep short and all turned for home.
Donaldson nursed his engine carefully all the way
back, while we all stuck around to make sure nobody
spotted his trouble and took a sudden crack at him.
He landed safely at Takali, after a slow ride home.

On the following day Johnnie Farmer and I
went to look for an alleged German bomber south
and east of Malta and found him forty miles out to sea.
But it was no Jerry. The Beauforts from Luqa had
gone east to sock a Rommel-bound convoy and this

poor devil had been pasted with flak from an enemy merchantman or escort vessel. When we found him he was streaming smoke and seemed to be in trouble. But he kept flying and landed at Luqa, though he couldn't get his undercart down and had to light on his belly with a badly overheated engine.

Two days later, after a routine patrol on the 25th, sixteen of us went back to Sicily, eight of 249 and eight from our companion mob. The trip brought us no luck, but cost us one of the gang, Micky Butler. We went in over Scaramia at dusk, Wing Commander Donaldson, Hether, Willie, Georgia, Shewell, Bryden, Micky, and I, and were on our way out when Micky suddenly called: "I gotta bale!" into the RT. Another minute passed. We were all watching Micky and his ship seemed to be completely under control. Then the same call came again: "I gotta bale out!" and some wag, thinking Micky must be kidding, for he was still in formation and seemed to be going strong, croaked: "All right, Micky! Go ahead and bale!" Just as he said it, Butler's Spitfire shoved its nose down and went into a vertical dive. It never came out. Whether Micky'd been fighting jammed controls, or what, none of us will ever know. Poor old Mick! He'd flown bombers for months from Britain, plastering German and Italian war installations, before transferring to Spits and coming to Malta, where he'd been a popular guy with everybody.

The Dog came back and spent the next three days with me and I didn't fly again until the 29th, when I flipped around the island for the better part of an hour, just split-assing around to keep my hand in. Nothing but a routine scramble on the 30th, when Ops thought seven or eight fighters were coming to leave cards. We stayed up about forty minutes, Giddy Giddings and I, until Ops told us to pancake. Shewell and I got the same kind of call the next day while we were up fooling around, dogfighting each other. Ten Jerry small jobs were supposed to be on the way and we were sent to intercept them at the eastern end of the island, over Kalfrana Bay. I guess they must have thought better of it, for we never saw them. That ended August. Things were getting pretty damned dull. In the whole month I'd destroyed only one German, the day I was shot down myself, and had been credited with a one-third share in another. Oh, well. You might keep catching the Dog, but you'd never pick up a case of the twitch in this kind of going!

Early in September, thanks to the accursed Dog, I missed out on the best offensive show the Malta Spits put on during the Big Lull, a huge sweep in which the boys shot the hell out of Jerry on the ground. What luck!

The Great Day was September 4th, when Group Captain Churchill led the whole Malta Spitfire force across to Sicily for a mass attack on Comiso, Biscari and Gela airdromes, with two purposes in view—to shoot the places up and to make the enemy come up and fight. It was our first real show of strength. I wouldn't have missed it for a million, Dog or no Dog. But all I could do was sit around and watch the clock, wondering how the boys were getting along. They were doing fine!

When the force reached Sicily it split up and went to work on all three fields at once. Bedlam was let loose everywhere. At Comiso the Jerry pilots ran to their ships and tried to get off the ground. There the lads from Luqa shot down three Ju 88s before they could get a hundred feet into the air. Everyone spun back in. One of the lads from our companion squadron at Takali, Parkinson, an Aussie D.F.C., knocked off a Ju 88 and an Me below 1,000 feet. Jim Ballantyne, a Canuck in the same outfit, destroyed an Me and shared a Dornier with Wing Commander Donaldson. Bob Seed and Scarlet Shewell each destroyed an 88 on the ground and Georgia nipped an 87 at Gela, where Junior Moody destroyed a Cant. Willie the Kid damaged a couple. The party was so fast and furious that it was all hell trying to keep tabs on who shot what. Caught flatfooted, the Huns and Eyeties lost twenty-two aircraft in a matter of minutes, on the ground and in the air. If the enemy had radio locator on Sicily, it must have been out of kilter that day! His ack-ack wasn't much better, but it scored one lucky, tragic shot, putting a burst into Group Captain Churchill's engine. The ship burst into flames and the group captain spun in, right near the Biscari airdrome. When the war ends, our side should erect a monument over his grave to commemorate a daringly conceived and courageously led raid. But for this, it was a grand show, its only other casualty an American lad from Halfar, who crash-landed after being hit in the engine and was taken prisoner.

The humiliated Huns and Eyeties picked up the pieces and shot a big fighter sweep at us on the 6th. That day de Nencrede and Bob Middlemiss were shot down, though both lads baled, wounded, and were fished out of the Mediterranean. This was another party I missed, thanks to Dog-grogginess, though I'd done a routine scramble the day before and gone Hun-hunting with Hether, Shewell, and Budd over the seaplane base at Syracuse in the evening. Our lads were led by McElroy and Bob copped it first, when two Me's dived on his tail before our guys had climbed into the fray. I guess the Jerry pilots must have been told to get in there and fight, after what happened the day before. Although badly wounded in the right hand and arm, Bob was able to roll over on his back and tumble out. He got down okay, inflated his dinghy and shinned into it, but drifted around for more than five hours before a searching Spitfire found him, several miles east of Zonkor Point and sent the rescue launch out to get him. The poor devil was in bad shape when the boys found him.

De Nencrede picked up *his* package while attacking a Schmitt and was hit by a cannon shell in the middle of a roll. His engine began smoking to beat hell, so he baled. When he was picked up the doc in the rescue launch extracted a shell splinter which had driven up through de Nencrede's right eyelid, pinning it back to the brow, miraculously missing the pupil. The guy was flying again before I left Malta. We got no Jerries that day.

A few petty scrambles and small sweeps were the order of the next four days. Nothing happened, though we'd dared the birds at Comiso and Biscari to come up and fight. On the 11th we tried a new wrinkle, sending three Hurri-bombers over to Sicily, escorted by an even dozen Spitters, six from 249, six from our neighbor squadron at Takali. Wing Commander Donaldson led us and Seed, Georgia, Scarlet, Giddy, and I made up the rest of the gang. We circled over Filfola at 8,000 feet, then made off for Sicily, climbing to 18,000 on the way. The drome at Gela was our objective and when we came over the coast we orbited under a cloud bank while the Hurries made ready to dive. Right then two Me's appeared. The Hurricanes peeled off in a hell of a hurry, diving for Gela. Two got right in and dropped their bombs smack on the runways. The third pilot got his ideas tangled and laid his eggs on the town by mistake. Meanwhile the fighters were milling around up high, waiting for the Me's to come down and do something about it, but they stayed where they were; so, as the bombers came out, we formed up and set sail for home.

Somebody promptly spotted a bomb dangling under a wing of one of the Hurries, which had un-loaded on the field. You can bet there was plenty of wigwagging and pointing going on until the dis-coverer was sure the Hurri-pilot had heard the bad news. For about fifteen minutes the poor bloke worked like mad on his release gear, but the damned thing hung on tenaciously. Malta was in sight by this time and the pilot was just about ready to bale—when WHAM! The bomb released itself, just as the Hurricane passed above a fleet of Maltese fishing smacks! It exploded right in among the boats and threw plenty of Mediterranean at the crews, who were mad as hell and couldn't imagine why their own pals were bombing them. Fortunately there were no casualties. Even so, the local authorities complained about the "unwarranted attack" and a good deal of explaining had to be done. Once the real story was told, however, everybody laughed it off—including the bombed fishermen!

On the 13th we were still hunting trouble, but finding none. Hether, Willie, Georgia, Johnnie Farmer, and I took a flip across to Sicily and went down to take a look at Pachino Strip, a reserve drome where Jerry was reported to be keeping a few aircraft. We didn't see a thing and nobody tried to interfere with us. The next two days were washouts.

Hether and I went up to intercept eight Me's which came over for a look-see on the 16th and we kicked the ball around for nearly an hour, during which one of the gentlemen, member of a trio which had jumped on me at 14,000 feet, put a burst through my right wing and a bullet through the tail stabilizer. Hether tangled with the other five, got a shot at one and damaged it. Things were certainly going fine for me—missing all the good shows, getting shot up on the little puky parties. I was beginning to itch with impatience for action and when 249 was washed out for the day on the 17th, I dropped over to the neighbors and asked if I could fly with them, just to change the luck. They said: "Okay, come on in and be our guest pilot, toots!" and I got into one scramble in which, as usual lately, I got no action, but might easily have connected with a broken neck. When I was slipping back into Takali, damned if my flaps would go down! I pulled up and went around again, working at the lever, but nothing happened. Takali is a pretty small field for one of these Twentieth Century Limited landings, so I flipped across to Luqa and landed, flaps up, like a runaway horse. The Spitter and I braked to a stop in time, but we landed galloping. I stayed at Luqa while a couple of erks fixed the flaps, then beetled home, no better off for my day in strange company.

A four-man sweep on the 19th cost us one of our seasoned pilots, Peter Peters. Pete, Hether, Georgia, and I were sent to sweep over Cape Scaramia at 20,000, and while we were· messing around Sicily a bunch of Macchis tried to gang us. One of them caught him with a wild-eyed deflection shot, clear out of nowhere, and Pete never knew what hit him. He simply fell off the end of our line-abreast formation and dived into the sea from 20,000 feet. Another of the well-liked guys gone home! The rest of us had no luck. A lousy show.

McElroy evened the score the next day by copping an Me on a four-man scramble against nine yellow-noses. Hiskens, Hogarth, and Yates were the others engaged, and Hiskens and Hogy both came home with their ships riddled. For the moment 249 seemed to be off the beam. Too much Malta Dog around. Pretty damned near everybody in the outfit was flying with black spots in front of his eyes all the time.

On the 21st eight of us, led by Timber Wood, dealt a hand against a raid of more than twenty fighters. We tried everything in the book, from head-on attacks to chasing them all the way home to Sicily, but not a mother's son of us got so much as a burst in on them. On the 24th I went to Pachino Strip again, with Wing Commander Donaldson, Shewell, and Bryden. Ops had told us to expect to find a few Jerries in the air, but we didn't see a sign of them. On the way out, however, we spotted what seemed to be a few small merchantmen in a bay near the strip and came home to report the discovery. Ops promptly called for a dozen Spitfires to go and shoot them up, but when the boys arrived they discovered they'd walked into a decoy job. The damned things were flak ships and, as the Spits peeled off and went down to shoot up the harmless merchantmen, the ships opened up with ack-ack and gave the lads hell. Everybody got back, but a thin time was had by all.

As far as I was concerned, I'd come to the conclusion I must be stale. Nothing seemed to work right. I couldn't even pick a camouflaged flak ship any more. But the 25th was another day. By the time night fell I was back in the groove—and about time!

Hether and I scrambled to meet eighteen Me's, with half a dozen other guys coming up behind to join us. The two of us went up to better than 20,000 feet, hanging on our props. The Huns were just arriving and I promptly picked out two who were riding close together and attacked. Not five seconds after we started the melee, I had the first one, catching him with a deflection shot from the starboard side. I must have got him in the oxygen bottles, for he blew into a million pieces. The other laddie tried to pull up into a steep climb, but I came right in under him, pulled the stick back and went along with him. I got my sights on his engine and let him have a two-second burst. The last I saw of him his engine was spewing black smoke and he was high-tailing toward Sicily. He was counted Damaged.

I looked around for Hether and saw him off in the distance, scrapping merrily with four Schmitts. "Want a hand, Hether?" I called into the mike. "I'll be okay!" he sang back. So I moseyed off in the general direction of a couple of 109s, two or three miles away, looking around to make sure nobody was getting ready to polish *me* off. Looking below, I saw an Me closing in on a Spitter for a sitting-duck kill. Hurriedly I called: "Spitfire flying west, alone. Break left! Messerschmitt on your tail!" As I yelled, I peeled down after the Me and from an angle and a distance of 250 yards slapped a one-and-a-half seconds squirt into his gas tank. He burst into flames, flicked over and spun down. Ernie Budd was happy to confirm him for me— it was Ernie's tail I'd wiped clean! Budd had been on his way up to join us, as were Squadron Leader Wood, Al Yates, Sandy Sanderson, Junior Moody, and Red Bryden.

So I'd copped a couple of Jerries again and damaged another, right when fortune seemed at its lowest ebb and I'd been wondering if I'd forgotten the trick. It was my first bit of luck since August 3rd, when I'd shared a bomber with Wynn and Jonesy while we were up west escorting the navy.

Jerry's fighter sweeps were getting bigger and peskier, a sure sign that something was brewing. Night bombings were stepping up. More alerts were sounding in Valetta and around the island. Even though nothing major happened during the dying days of September and early October, bar a couple of dud scrambles and an almost equally dud sweep over Comiso, Syracuse and Scaramia, the old feeling of something-coming-up was getting into our bones again. The bones didn't lie. Action *was* coming up again. And when it came it would be the real McCoy!

CHAPTER VIII

"May Day! May Day! May Day!"

As it had been in July, so it was in October. You could feel it coming. Instinctively you knew that the enemy was going to make another attempt to blow Malta into the sea, to finish the razing of its towns, force the surrender of its people and drive the British out of their only remaining mid-Mediterranean stronghold. Don't ask me *how* you know these things. You simply do. It wasn't just a handful of Spitter pilots who were seeing things, or dreaming them, or getting pixillated. Every man and woman on the whole damned island *knew* that the Huns were about to come at us again and try to finish the job.

How did everybody feel about it? I wouldn't know. We guys on the airfields lived pretty much to ourselves. You can't be on call from daylight to dark, seven days a week and every week, and spend much time being a social lion downtown—and the social life of Malta was no hell at any time, if only for the reason that you can't throw many parties when you

can't offer the guests a bite to eat. But some of the
boys used to get around here and there, with the
people from Ops, with military and civilian Britishers,
and with the Maltese. They all seemed to be hearing
the same story—better the Blitz then the strain of
waiting for it.

The truth of the matter is that the August convoy
hadn't solved any riddles for the island. It takes a hell
of a lot of grub and clothing to take care of 250,000
people, and Lord Gort had been dishing it out
damned sparingly. For a long time quite a bit of stuff
had been freighted across from Gozo in boats to sup-
plement the Malta convoy diet, but the finish of
summer put an end to that. Pretty nearly all the pigs
and goats had been killed for food—and when you
kill a Maltese goat you are shutting off the milk
supply at its source. Rations were away down, not
just for civilians, but for soldiers and airmen as well.
As a matter of fact, food was issued pretty evenly all
round. True, the fliers had to be kept fed, but you
couldn't starve the civilian population and expect the
Maltese to keep punching—and if you couldn't keep
the Maltese in line, how were you going to hold the
island? Not that they ever became a problem. They
were too damned mad for that. Even so, they had to
be given the breaks too; the same breaks everybody
else got.

You couldn't have called it a pretty picture that

fall. Everybody's physical pep was away below par. The combination of the summer climate and vegetables grown in overfertilized soil had the place Dog-ridden from Valetta to Kalfrana Bay. Offhand my guess would be that the new German-Italian attempt to knock us over came as a relief, gave everybody on the island something to think about, something to get hot under the collar about. That was a damned sight better for everybody than waiting for the convoys that couldn't get through, and nothing had slipped into the harbor since the badly mauled merchantmen and the torpedoed tanker had made it in August. It wasn't just the Spitter guys and the rest of the RAF who were glad to see Jerry getting busy again. Everybody was. Nothing like a good blitz to put you on your toes!

249's luck was still out and we lost two ships and pilots before the gong even rang for the main bout. That was on October 3rd. The fire didn't really get going for almost a week after that. But Jerry's Fighter sweeps were growing stronger and more bothersome, although he hadn't gone back to daylight bombing yet.

Following a couple of routine scrambles earlier in the day, McElroy, Carter, Hogarth, and Gass went up to intercept seventeen Me's over the sea. Before they ever got into action an Me dived on Gass, who had fallen slightly behind the formation, and got him with one quick burst. In the melee proper Hogy's ship was badly shot up and the white streamer of his leaking glycol could be seen from the ground while he was still up high. He made an attempt to land on a new drome south of Luqa, undershot and hit a rock, off which he caromed into a building. They said he had fractured his skull and bruised his brain. His head had been badly grazed by a bullet and I guess the poor kid had tried to make a landing half-dazed. He died in hospital that night, one of the best guys Canada ever sent over to fly.

For quite a while that afternoon we thought three-quarters of the scramble had gone west, or missing, for when Mac landed alone he had no idea what had become of Pete Carter, his fourth man. Half an hour passed, then forty-five minutes. That's time, reckoned in terms of a Spitter's durability. Finally, just as we were giving up hope, a Spit came swooping in from the sea. It was Carter. "I chased the bastards damn nearly back to Sicily," he said. "But damned if I could get at them!"

That was how it began, Then, as before, things lulled again. Wing Commander Donaldson, Hether, Willie, and I tooled over to Sicily on the 5th, looking things over at Comiso and Gela. The dromes looked serenely quiet from the air, though Intelligence kept warning of considerable activity and we heard a flock of new Me's had flown in. We were all getting that anxious-seat feeling again, just as we'd had it in July.

Meanwhile the erks were getting every possible hour in on our ships, prettying-up for Jerry and the Eyeties.

What happened on the 9th was in the nature of a God-given break, if ever I got one. I was local-flying over Takali, testing my newly serviced Spit, when Ops slipped me the office that two Me's had sneaked in behind the island, on the south side, and were over Filfola, apparently snooping for ground defenses. I slung out in a wide arc, high and well to the south of Filfola and came sneaking down, between the two Germans and the sea. They were traveling line abreast at no more than a thousand feet when I dropped in on them. I went down and down, clean under the starboard fellow, and rolled up under him, giving him a quick burst into the engine. He pancaked right smack down on his belly on the island and flipped over onto his back. The crack killed the pilot and pranged the crate pretty badly. Number One.

The other fellow tried to circle away, but I stayed with him. He turned out to sea, then whipped back and crossed Filfola again. As he did I moved onto his starboard quarter and let him have it. The burst caught the gas tank and the ship blew up, complete with pilot. Number Two.

That lifted my Malta score in Aircraft Destroyed to twenty-one and a third, twenty-three and a third all told, counting Occupied France.

Just at dusk on the 9th, Louis de l'Ara pulled off

one of the best shows in Malta aerial history. Going up with one other pilot, Sergeant Stead, one of our latest batch of newcomers, Louis followed Ops's directions so accurately that he intercepted a sweep of eighteen Ju 88 bombers and played such hell with them that he shot one down and forced the others to unload their bombs in the sea. The Ju's were without fighter escort, and de l'Ara whipped in and out among them to his heart's content. Louis won the D.F.M. for a damned good show.

After two blank days, the 10th and 11th, we ran into a peck of trouble on the 12th. Eight of us scrambled, led by Timber Wood, to break up a raid of two Ju 88s escorted by forty Me's. Eight Spits from our neighbor squadron also were sent into the melee. While we were still 5,000 feet under the Jerries, a flock of the Schmitts dived and before we knew what was happening had picked off Carter and Hiskens. The poor devils didn't have a chance. It was over in a flash. The Huns bombed Gozo and killed eleven "neutral" civilians. A stinking day's work!

The next day things went better—a hell of a sight better for a change! The tip was out to expect big doings, and the wingco had us all out of our beds by 2:30 A.M. and down to dispersal soon after. The whole outfit was called. No Red Section stuff this time; no "Who's first off?" Every pilot in 249 from Timber down to the newest arrival was on deck in his Mae West, ready for the call.

It came at 4:30—just about daylight. "249 Squadron—SCRAMBLE!" Chairs went flying. Mugs of cocoa were dropped on the floor. You'd think a stick of bombs was just about to hit the roof the way that gang hoicked out of the hut and across the field, each to the nook where his own Spitter was waiting. We went off in fours, Hether, Willie, Shewell, and I leading, and if four guys ever went up perpendicularly in four Spitters, we were those guys: 28,000 feet was our destination and we arrived practically panting. As we got there we spotted the enemy in the half-light— fifteen bombers and at least eighty fighters. If this was what was building up, no wonder Ops had us out of bed early!

My damned RT went out of kilter just as I saw the raiders coming, and I couldn't say a word to warn my sidekicks. I simply peeled off from my inside port position and whammed down through the fighters onto the outside starboard Ju, the rear position in the V of bombers. As I went down I gave him a long burst in the starboard engine, right from the tail. It was no fancy deflection shot, but it took hold of the gentle-man just the same. The Ju broke formation and dived toward the sea, flaming. Nobody saw him hit, so he was only counted Damaged.

I promptly found myself playing host to about

twenty Messerschmitts, diving on me in a covey. I whipped around fast and broke right back through the middle of the whole bunch, every mother's son of them taking a crack at me as I went past, or so it seemed to me, sitting in the middle of a tracer fireworks show. As soon as I'd broken into the clear I whipped right round again onto their tails, only to discover that two of the Schmitts had whipped in behind me. I did another quick, tight whip-over behind them and got in a hurry-up deflection shot on the fellow on the port side. He was set up perfectly for just such a shot, almost exactly 300 yards away in the sights. That meant he'd take the whole load of cannon and machine guns, if I was on the bead. Luckily I was. The whole burst must have gone squarely into his tank and the engine. He blew just as if there'd been a charge of dynamite in the cockpit. Pieces were flying all around the sky. The fuselage burst into a sheet of flame. No question what happened to him!

I went into a steep climbing turn and after his running mate; up to the right and winging over to get him into my sights as he tried to maneuver around onto my tail. A one-second burst into the engine settled him. The hood flew off the cockpit, apparently jettisoned by the pilot. The engine began to spew smoke. He rolled onto his back and baled.

Right at that moment a Spitfire came spinning

past, just as the German pilot's parachute opened. A couple of nearby Me's, their pilots apparently thinking a Spitter flier had baled, promptly circled around the parachutist and, one after the other, gave him a traversing burst. The guy under the canopy went limp and hung dangling under the riddled chute, which quickly lost its airworthiness as the Huns sprayed it with lead. When last I saw the murdered German he was falling rapidly toward the sea.

That's German sportsmanship for you. The big shots of the Heinie Staff would call it realism, I imagine. . . . The only good enemy pilot is a dead pilot. True enough. A live pilot is worth half a dozen aircraft. But if that's Nazi realism, may God spare me from Nazism! To anybody who doesn't share my opinion all I can say is "Fine. But wait until *you* sit in an aeroplane cockpit, five miles above the world, and watch a helpless man murdered in his parachute!" If you don't boil, brother, and hate the living guts of every Hun-damned German, even though it's one of his own gang you've watched him kill, then there's something wrong with you! Christ! I damned nearly vomited in the cockpit, just watching the swine kill their own man! What would my feelings have been if the fellow under the parachute had been Hether, or Willie the Kid, or Bob Seed? Figure that one out, when you're feeling well disposed towards Germans.

The show wasn't over yet. Only four of the

bombers got through to Malta. They bombed Takali, laying two big eggs in the field. The rest went into Attard, the adjacent village, killing five Maltese and wounding quite a few others. I hooked up with the Ju's as they were climbing away after dive-bombing the field and village. I grabbed onto one from the starboard quarter, on a deflection angle, as I was diving and gave him every drop of ammunition I had left. It took him in the starboard wing-root, between the engine and fuselage. He streamed black, oily smoke and dived right into the deck.

While all this was going on my seat had broken loose, from all the fast pull-outs I'd been making. That last leap, down onto the 88, had been made at better than 500 miles an hour. One break in the luck —I'd got the RT working again. I told Takali I'd broken my seat and to have the crash wagon ready, as I could barely see over the fuselage. Takali said: "Okay. Come in and land!"

The landing was pretty good, although I had to crane my neck to the limit to see what I was doing. As soon as I'd taxied out of harm's way everybody came running over, obviously greatly concerned for my health and ready to lift a cripple out of the cock-pit. I couldn't figure why, until I discovered that the ground operator had mistaken my call. For "seat" she had heard "feet"!

That was a real show! Eleven bombers of a total

of fifteen failed to reach their objective at all, were either shot down or dropped their bombs in the sea, before turning tail for home. Eight Huns went to their last reward—which is okay by me! Who got them, I'll never know, because my own Malta string was running out and the score has never caught up with me. My own part of it accounted for two Me's and one Ju 88 Destroyed, one Ju 88 Damaged.

The 14th was my last day in the air over Malta. Just one scramble. But what a scramble!

It happened shortly after noon and the whole squadron, as on the 13th, was on immediate readiness, as was one full squadron at Luqa. Ops scrambled the works, to intercept eight Ju 88s and fifty fighters, and Hether, Giddings, Bryden, and I were the first four off, Hether leading. We zoomed right through to 20,000 and spotted the sweep coming in from the east end of the island a couple of thousand feet below us. Without waiting for the rest of 249 to get up to us, or for the Luqa boys to arrive, Hether led us right into the muss, head-on. He took Giddy with him to break up the bombers, while Red and I took on the fighters, to keep them away from the other pair.

As the action opened I spotted five fighters pulling up high, as if to get ready to dive on Giddy and Hether. I called into the mike: "Climb, Red! Keep those yellow-nosed bastards off Hether's tail!" and we soared up to 24,000 feet, just as the five Me's got there.

The Schmitts promptly peeled off and dived. I yelled: "Come on, Red! Down we go!" and away we went, right among the bombers, where a general mess-up was developing. We each picked a Ju. I took the one on the starboard rear position of the V and gave him a two-second burst from starboard, getting him in the old coffin corner—the starboard engine and gas tank. He burst into flame and went headlong toward the sea.

As I nabbed the bomber, Hether came whipping just under me, diving away from eight Me's on his tail. I went down in a hurry with them, right past my Flamer, and lashed into the leading Hun, just as he was going to let Hether have it. As I passed the burning bomber the rear gunner took a shot at me, peppering the port side of my fuselage and the port wing. I picked up about thirty bullet holes, I guess. Explosive bullets were snapping through the cockpit and one nicked the left middle finger of my throttle hand. Another stabbed my left forearm. What was more important and inconvenient at the moment, however, I'd picked up two Me's on my own tail and still had Hether to worry about.

I had to shoot in one hell of a hurry to clean Hether up and salvage my own neck, so I took a chance and tried a long shot, from about 450 yards from above and to port. I got the bastard in the engine and he dove for the sea, streaming smoke and shedding pieces. That was all right as far as it went, but while

I was busy on him, one of the Me's on my tail riddled my port wing like a sieve and put a couple of bullets through the perspex hood, right over my head, while the other Schmitt blasted my starboard wing full of holes. Things were warming up. Well, Hether was out in the clear again. That was something!

The old crate was still flying, so I climbed, heading for some place from which I could survey the battlefield. The wounded Spitter was finding the going rough, but we were still making pretty fair weather, full of holes though we were. I clambered up to 24,000 again, still after a couple of the Me's who had been trying to polish Hether off. I was just getting all set to take a bead on one of the gentlemen when a call for help came over the RT: "Anybody around Kalfrana Bay! Come give us a hand! Two of us are in a jam with twenty Me's!"

My own position was right above Kalfrana, so I rolled over and had a look down, to see a swell melee going on below. I went down vertically, hitting almost 600 mph in my riddled crate and at 14,000 feet pulled up under a Messerschmitt, just as he was all set to pot Willie the Kid. You might have guessed it would be Willie! That guy and I were always turning up when we needed each other most. No matter what happened, it always seemed to be Willie or Hether.

There wasn't a split-second to waste. Just as I pulled up from the dive and was going back up vertically I gave the son of a Hun a two-second burst and blew his whole left wing off at the root. He flicked over, and that was that. Willie's ship, shot to ribbons, was just about able to cart him home, no more.

Maybe I saved Willie's bacon, but in doing it I sure singed my own—fell right into the trap that everybody walks into sooner or later, no matter how much he coaches himself not to. There's a simple axiom for it: "Always look behind you before you go in to attack." Well, I didn't. I'd been so damned intent on the guy in my sights and on Willie's tail that I'd forgotten I had a tail of my own. I soon had reason to remember it.

Just as I shot Willie's pal down, another Me nailed me from behind. He got me right in the belly of the Spit. A chunk of cannon shell smashed into my right heel. Another went between my left arm and body, nicking me in the elbow and ribs. Shrapnel spattered into my left leg. The controls were blasted to bits. The throttle was jammed wide open and there I was in a full-power spin, on my way down from somewhere around 18,000 feet. I threw the hood away and tried to get out, but the spin was forcing me back into the seat. "This is it," I said to myself. "This is what it's like when you know you're going to die."

I didn't panic. If anything, I was resigned to it. It had been a good show, all things added up. I'd proved my point, here over Malta. I'd lived. I could die if I had to. What the hell! This was the way I'd always wanted to go, when the time came. Looking back from here it seems as if there was a definite space, spinning in that cockpit, in which I had completely resigned myself to the big smack that was just a matter of instants ahead. Then I snapped out of it and began to struggle again.

The engine was streaming flame by this time, but somehow I managed to wriggle my way out of the cockpit and out onto the port wing, from which I could bale into the inside of the spin. By the time I got out onto the wing I was down to 2,000 feet. At about 1,000 I managed to slip off. Before I dared pull the ripcord I must have been around 500. The chute opened with a crack like a cannon shell and I found myself floating gently down in the breeze, the damnedest experience in contrasts I shall ever have in this life.

I caught my breath, then pulled off a glove and dropped it, to get some idea of the distance between me and the sea. A breeze caught it and the glove went up past my face. I heard myself laugh like a fool. I tugged off my flying boots and dropped them. Just as I did I hit the water.

Meanwhile Bob Seed had been sitting in a ringside seat and had given Ops three *May Days* for Beurling. He circled around me as I spun down and called as soon as he saw me bale, sticking around until I'd landed safely on old Mother Mediterranean and

**BY THE TIME I GOT OUT ONTO THE WING I WAS DOWN TO
2,000 FEET**

had fished out my rubber dinghy. A couple of Me's had been hovering around like vultures, he told me later. "So I stuck around to save your useless goddam Canadian hide," he said. That was next day, over in hospital.

I only floated around in the dinghy for a matter of twenty minutes, but the bottom was red with Beurling blood by the time the rescue launch came along. They hoicked me ashore in Kalfrana Bay, where the MO tied me up and shipped me to hospital. Two hours after scrambling from Takali I was on a wheel-stretcher, on my way to the operating room! As I passed out under the anaesthetic I could hear another dogfight getting going. The Blitz was in full spate—and I was out of it! I'd have to be content with the score for a while, and call it a ball game!

CHAPTER X

End of an Odyssey

(ROBERTS: For the record, another medal-ribbon had been sewn on young Beurling's tunic before he was shot down, the diagonal stripes of the Distinguished Flying Cross. It covered his exploits up to and including September 25, 1942, and news of the award reached Malta just as the October blitz was beginning to roll in high gear. The citation reads:

> Since being awarded a Bar to the D.F.M., this officer has shot down a further three hostile aircraft, bringing his total victories to twenty. One day in September (1942) he and another pilot engaged four enemy fighters. In ensuing combat Pilot Officer Beurling destroyed two of them. A relentless fighter whose determination and will has won the admiration of his colleagues, this officer has set an example in keeping with the highest traditions of the RAF.

"How do you like all that 'tradition' stuff?" I asked, putting the citation down.

"I could use a couple of hot dogs," the young man answered. "What say we send for a flock?"

We rang for them. While we waited, Beurling said: "Lemme see that paper a minute."

I passed it over and he sat reading. Then he grinned.

"Something missing here," he chuckled. "They clean forgot the piece of a bomber, the one I shared with Jonesy and Georgia the day we went out to fly with the navy. No allowance for cold meat, huh?"

According to private advices from Malta, or from people who were around at the time, Beurling was not what could be called the ideal patient. What was the idea of fussing around with a lot of skin grazes and a little bit of a bullet hole in his heel? Couldn't they put some kind of guard over it, to protect it from rubbing, or something? You know, doc, they need me up there. The Hun's raising hell. It isn't fair to the other guys I should be here. Hell, they need all the help they can get. Cripes, doc, it isn't fair to me either. Can't you get me outa here?

"Doc" was Colonel Davidson of Montreal, and by all accounts the young man ran him ragged. At first the MO used to grin and say: "We'll have you fixed up in no time, George. Keep -your shirt on." Then he began to bring in such items as infection and drainage and intimate it might take a little time. That would bring the kid bolt upright demanding: "Time! What do you mean, time? How much time?" With that the colonel would begin to hedge and mutter phrases like "Oh, couple of weeks, maybe!" and George's face would be wreathed in disgust as he answered: "Sure. Fine. Couple of weeks. Couple of weeks, the show'll be over and half the squadron'll be dead. Have a heart, doc. I'm okay. You know I'm okay." Which is all very well. Unfortunately you can't live on siege diet and be a living monument to the Malta Dog for weeks on end and be a quick-healer, which probably explains why Pilot Officer Beurling was still crutch-ridden come January, 1943, the bullet hole in his heel still open.

The kid needed his vitamins and was only then beginning to reap the benefits of getting them back. Meanwhile, back home in a Canadian hospital, he was not what might be called a tractable patient.)

It was certainly hell to lie flat on your back in hospital and listen to the biggest blitz of all going on right over your head. I could hear the racket even before I had completely shaken the anaesthetic, and they told me the next day the first question I asked was "How long, doc?" . . . "And how long did the doc say, sister?" I asked the nurse. She simply smiled and said I'd better talk to the MO about that myself.

Hether, Willie, and Al Yates came over to see me on the 16th and talking to them didn't help a bit. The scrambles were coming oftener and were bigger than ever. Jerry was coming over in wave after wave, hour after hour, from daylight to dusk. Junior Moody had copped a Ju 88 on the 15th. Squadron Leaders Wood of 249 and Stevens, the D.S.O., D.F.C. and Bar who commanded the other Takali outfit, both had their Spits badly shot up in the same show, Stevens while flying with 249, just to help out. Red Bryden had been badly wounded by a cannon shell and had baled out. He was abed one floor below my ward. A couple of lads from other Spit squadrons had been shot down that day. One had crash-landed at Takali; the other had baled into the sea. Both were okay. Giddy Giddings had destroyed an Me.

"Funny thing," Hether said as the gang all sat around on the bed, talking blitz, "the Eyeties are giving us more trouble than Jerry. Isn't that the way you find it, Willie?"

The Kid agreed. "It's the damned Reggianes, George," he said. "They're going like hell. Flying like mad. Split-assing all over the sky. And staying to fight, what I mean."

"Blimy!" Hether came in. "We nearly forgot to tell you a bunch of Me's shot up Takali today, whisking around not ten feet off the ground. Some of the chaps in the other mob had their aircraft shot up, trying to get into the air and do battle. Jim Ballantyne took an awful pasting, I hear."

This was the kind of talk to give a guy the twitch. Before another couple of days were gone I was sneaking from bed to a window, just to sit there and watch the sky; then I'd go back to bed and wait for the colonel to come around, to give him another argument about getting out. Couldn't he fix it so I could work with the boys, daytimes, and come back to the hospital to sleep and get new bandages?

Colonel Davidson was a great guy, very quiet-spoken, but a kidder. He was always going to have me out and around in a couple of days, but I couldn't get any nearer than that. That was great stuff, particularly when your friends came in around teatime to tell you about a big scramble they'd just come back from: hundred-plus stuff, the biggest Malta had ever seen.

The night bombings were getting to be terrific. The whole ruddy island was taking an awful pounding—Valetta, Luqa, Attard, even the village where the hospital was. Some of the stuff fell not two hundred yards from the building where we were quartered—and that's no way to be wakened out of a deep sleep at three in the morning. Give me a scramble any time, where you can do something about it yourself.

Meanwhile I was spending practically all my waking hours in the bathtub. If you'd seen me when the crew of the rescue launch hauled me in! The last Jerry who polished me off—the guy I forgot to look for on my tail—had hit my oil (the bastard hadn't missed *anything!*) and the stuff had come spewing back into the cockpit. I was properly drenched with it, in my hair, everywhere. It took a three-day course of hot baths and scrubbings by a hospital orderly before you could see my face coming through the film.

I soon had company from 249. Johnnie Farmer. Johnnie, the lucky stiff, baled out of a power dive, going about 450 mph, with his controls shot to blazes. Then he'd made a slight miscalculation in his relief on finding himself loose from his ship and pulled the ripcord while he was falling like Billy-be-damned. You have to wait for these things. Leave it to nature. If you bale at 450, then you're doing 450, or thereabouts, yourself. But if you give old gravity a chance you slow right down to a top speed of 118.6 miles an hour, and when the chute opens you don't get much of a jerk. Well, Johnnie forgot his schoolbooks and pulled the ripcord as soon as he was clear of the ship. The snap of the chute opening dislocated his shoulders and gave Johnnie a slight rupture. On top of that he'd broken an arm, somewhere along the line. So he wasn't a very comfortable guy when they carted him into the ward on a shutter.

The real lucky guy on the ward, however, was Art Roscoe, a Yank from the other Takali squadron, who'd been with 249 for a while when he first came out from England. A cannon shell had sliced right through Art's cockpit and through Art as well, entering his right breast, just below the shoulder, smashing his collarbone and going out through his back. Getting home as best he could he had crash-landed on Takali and burst into flames, but the smack had tossed him out onto a wing unconscious. A couple of erks had run into the fire and pulled him off the flaming wing!

The place was beginning to fill up with Spitter pilots. But everybody came bearing the same tale. We were handing it back to Jerry five for one. He might be playing hell, but he was paying a price for it—and not many Huns or Eyeties were getting a chance to bale.

Early evening we always fought the day's battles

over again in the ward. If Hether didn't get over, then
Willie would be there, or maybe Scarlet and Georgia.
No doubt about it, the going was tougher than ever
before. Hundred-plus German-Italian sweeps were
getting to be run-of-the-mill. But Ops was ticking like
a clock and most of the time there was ample warning
and our guys would be up there to meet them, way
out to sea, sometimes having good enough luck to turn
'em all back. But you could see the strain was telling
on them—signs of the twitch here and there. You can
take only so much in this business, and plenty of guys
had taken it long ago. Yet it was on the old-timers you
had to rely in the tough going. A couple of newcomers
had been knocked off during the early days of the
blitzing. No time to get to know the climate and dress
for it. But 249 was going strong. Still the fightingest
squadron in the RAF. Timber Wood had bagged a
couple more Jerries. Hether had chalked up two or
three Damageds—"But I'm missing you, mutt!" he
said. "Never was a team could get up there as fast as
we could. We'd be in our element in this show!" The
old cucumber! No twitch there!

I think it was on October 25th that Air Vice-
Marshal Park, the air officer commanding on Malta,
came over to hospital to see me. I think he started out
by telling me I'd been given the D.S.O., but I'm not
sure. Then he went on to say he had a message from
London. The Canadian government was asking that I

be sent home on leave and maybe to give a hand with recruiting and tell people the score, the way the fighter pilots see it.

I said: "I know, sir. But Colonel Davidson said I'd be fit to fly in a couple of weeks. I better stay, until this show's over anyway."

"Never believe a word a medical officer tells you, Beurling," the AOC answered. "They haven't enough to do with their time, so they go round making up damned lies to tell their patients. The real office on this business is that you won't be flying again for a couple of months at least."

That was a wallop. Right on the button. I'd been living from day to day telling the gang I'd be back in there with them any minute. But a couple of months! Cripes! "Okay, sir," I said. "Guess I might as well take a ride!" And that was that. So long, Malta.

(ROBERTS: "You forgot something, George," I said. "The AVM told you about the D.S.O. What was in the citation this time?"

"You tell me," said George. "I'll bet you've got it right there among the papers. All right. Go ahead. Read the damn thing!"

"Remember you asked for it," I said. "For a bunch of Englishmen the RAF gets pretty sentimental about a guy like you." The citation read:

Pilot Officer Beurling has destroyed a further six enemy aircraft, bringing his total victories to twenty-eight. During one sortie on October 13th (1942) he shot down a Ju-88 and two Me-109s. The following day, in a head-on attack on enemy Bombers, he destroyed one of them before he observed his leader being attacked by an enemy Fighter. Although wounded, Pilot Officer Beurling destroyed the Fighter; then climbing again . . . although his aircraft was hit by enemy fire . . . he shot down another Fighter before his own aircraft was so damaged that he was forced to abandon it. He descended safely onto the sea and was rescued. This officer's skill and daring are unexcelled.

"He descended safely onto the sea, covered with engine oil!" George chuckled. "And they still won't have any part of that 88 I shared with Jonesy and Georgia. No justice, is there?"

"No justice," I said. "So you went back to Canada!")

Two days after the AOC's visit, Timber Wood came over to the hospital in the squadron car to tell me I'd be leaving for Gib that night: how about coming over to Takali and the mess to say good-bye and collect your stuff?

"The good-byes won't be too hard to take," Timber said. "You'll have lots of company. Your pals Hether and Willie the Kid, to name two."

Even so it wasn't as easy as you might think, saying so-long to guys like Scarlet Shewell, Bob Seed, Georgia, Junior Moody, Giddy, Smoky Joe, Timber himself, and a flock of others who'd ridden around with me in some tough corners. They'd be staying and taking it. I'd be getting out, going home, back to the place where I'd shipped on munition ships to get into the show. She'd been a tough old siege. In little more than three months 249 had lost Harry Kelly, Tommy Tompkins, Gilbert, Chuck Ramsay, Berkeley-Hill, Jean Paradis, Smitty, Pete Peters, Gass, Hogarth, Hiskens, Pete Carter, and Micky Butler, all killed or missing. That alone is more than a squadron's pilot strength. Others had been wounded and were out of action: Middlemiss, de Nencrede, Mac MacLean, Johnnie Farmer, Red Bryden, myself. Old 249 had rolled up the score that summer. We were well over the 300 mark in Enemy Aircraft Destroyed, by that time. But some damned good pilots had footed the bill.

That evening we moved over to Luqa, ready to leave. Rip Mutch of 249 and Al Yates were both there ahead of Hether, Willie, and me. Wingco Donaldson was another who was coming along. From the other Takali squadron Eddie Glazebrooke, another Montrealer, and Sergeant "Bye-Bye" Bye, an English fellow, were on hand. Spence and Davies from Luqa, both Canucks, Sergeant Penny and a couple of Aussies from the same place, or Halfar, guys I didn't know very well, though we'd flown in plenty of mix-ups together. All told, twenty-six Malta pilots were going back. Soon after the 249 crowd arrived, Art Roscoe, my next-

THE PILOT BEGAN TO POUR COAL TO ALL HIS THROTTLES.
THE BIG SHIP JUMPED TO IT . . .

door neighbor in hospital turned up, looking pretty seedy, but cheerful. Four women, one English and three Maltese, would make the trip to Gib with us, plus two small babies. Three civilian men, all government officials of one kind or another, were going along. Counting the six-man crew, thirty-nine of us would be aboard the big Liberator when we pulled out. Then the weather soured . . .

The flight lieutenant who was skippering the Lib said: "Sorry, but you'll have to wait. It's clear out east. So I'm hopping to Alexandria instead, to pick up a load of freight." He pushed off for Alex and we all sat around the Luqa mess, with nothing to do but wait for our ship's return. I never put in a longer drag of waiting in my life, sitting right in the middle of a war, waiting to kiss it good-bye—watching the Spitters go zooming up, hearing the alert, listening to the crump of Jerry bombs, the racket of ack-ack at night. News came over from Takali that Giddy Giddings had crash-landed, killing a couple of Maltese who were running across the drome. He'd crashed trying to duck them; smashed his left wrist when he ground-looped. Smoky Joe Lowry had shot down an Me to add another notch to 249's mounting score. You heard the bulletins and you hated the idea of leaving—you with a pair of crutches under your armpits and a plaster cast on your foot!

The Lib came back from Alex the night of the

31st and at three A.M. on the 1st of November we were away, heading for the open country up west while there were no enemy fighters about. His night bombers had jobs of their own to do; they wouldn't be bothering us.

The big Liberator flew along cozily and soon you began to know you were in another world. Down below, on the African coast, we could see the sheen of lighted cities. As day dawned we flew along under clear skies, over a peaceful blue sea. Willie wandered back and yelled in my ear: "Whatever became of the war? Remember?" Hether was full of the old zing, laughing and talking, telling us what would be what as soon as the Hetherington hit Blighty. "Going to be tough on the British maidens when this gang gets in!" grinned Willie. The old Lib just plugged along. We'd be getting in soon.

Around Algiers we cut away from the African coast and across the sea toward Gibraltar. As we did, the clouds came lower and rain spattered against the windows. The going wasn't very rough, however, though we were bucking the wind. The closer to Gib, the lower the clouds. By the time we could see the Rock we were only about a thousand feet above the sea, just under the heavy muck. Gibraltar told the cockpit to swing out over the Straits, to the Atlantic side and make a north-to-south landing on the only strip there's room for between the Rock and the Spanish border.

We circled Gibraltar and began to settle down toward the runway. As we came in behind the Rock the ship was caught in new. eddies, caused by the action of the air around the huge rock pile itself. Our wheels didn't touch the runway until we were almost at the middle. Things didn't look so good. I sat there praying for the sound of gunned engines and began to peel out of my heavy flying coat.

The pilot began to pour coal in a hurry to all his throttles. The big ship jumped to it and picked up speed. When we went into the clear, off the end of the runway, we must have been making close to a hundred, and chances are we might have been okay if we'd taken our climb easy. We stalled at forty feet and dived into the sea!

As we stalled, I flung open an escape door right by my back seat, and just as we hit the water, before the big wallop hit us, I dived out. Two or three others followed right behind me. But at least half our passenger list was trapped in the cabin. Then, perhaps half a minute after the impact, the ship broke apart.

The first person I saw was Art Roscoe, hanging onto a chunk of wreckage. His fractured collarbone made swimming impossible. The crew had broken out of the cockpit and a couple of rubber dinghies had floated out. Half a dozen survivors who couldn't swim were loaded into the life rafts. I hung around looking for people to help, trying to find Hether and Willie and Rip Mutch, but couldn't see a sign of any of them. They, with Eddie Glazebrooke and eight or nine others, had been trapped in the ship, or killed by the impact of the blow when we hit the water. A bunch of army lads on the beach had seen us whisk over their heads and into the water, only 200 yards offshore, and plunged in, swimming out to help. Somebody yelled: "Better get ashore, if you can make it!" and I started dog-paddling in, the best I could do with a cast-encased foot.

As soon as the people on the shore saw the club foot they grabbed me and shoved me onto a stretcher. I kept saying: "I'm okay. Get somebody else!" But I might as well have been yelling in the middle of the desert. First thing I knew the stretcher was being hoicked into an ambulance and I was on my way to hospital and bed.

Gradually the news began to come through— fifteen people dead or missing. All the male civilians had been killed. One of the Maltese women had been killed in the crash and the Englishwoman had died on the way to hospital. Both babies were drowned. By nightfall the bad news was almost all in. Glazebrooke, Spence, and Davies of Luqa were gone. Rip Mutch was dead—Hether and Willie the Kid had both gone west.

I lay abed that night and looked out the window on the lights of Gibraltar. So this was how it had to end. You fly and you fight and you live for the minute, and you team up with guys who know nothing about you and about whom you know nothing. All you know is that the other guy is full of guts and does the job.

Then the break comes and you all fly away together, each to go his own way at the journey's end, but each with something to share with the others that none of you will ever forget. Then this . . .

I'd never go roaring up to 28,000 again with Hether, both of us proud as hell that we could beat any team in 249 to get up where the Jerries were. I'd never wipe another Hun off Willie's tail, or bawl him out for cruising around watching a Flamer spiral down. There wasn't any Hether. And there wasn't any Willie.

(ROBERTS: There were no more blitzes at Malta. All through October and into November the Spitter guys from Takali, from Luqa and Halfar knocked the Luftwaffe down and turned its bombers back, carrying on the traditions—that ten Jerries and Eyeties must go down for every Spitter that hit the sea. In eight days alone, of which Beurling's 13th and 14th of October, 1942, were two, a hundred enemy aircraft were destroyed or damaged by the RAF at Malta. Then Montgomery set about rolling up the coast, chasing Rommel and the Afrika Korps into Tripolitania and on toward Tunis. The Luftwaffe called it a day. And Malta had saved a great part of that day.

One night in November, while Valetta slept, a convoy of merchantmen and tankers slipped silently into Grand Harbour. When the "250,000 prisoners" awakened, ready to go about the chores of the day, the siege had been lifted. The final act had been played by the merchant navy and the fleet. But the stage had been cleared for their arrival by Yanks from Georgia and Texas, policemen from Wolverhampton, downy-cheeked kids from the Home Counties and hearty lads from Yorkshire, by Aussies and New Zealanders, by French Canadians and "guys" from the prairies, by youngsters who'd traveled the seven seas as deckhands on munition ships, for the chance to get in there and fight. It had been defended, too, by 250,000 men and women who were hopping mad and never knew the meaning of the verb "to quit."

On Malta they did know the meaning of Total War.)

Epilogue

I first met George Beurling in November 1943 at Biggin Hill fighter field in Kent, south of London. I was stationed there with 401 Squadron RCAF, part of 126 Wing. I already knew plenty about him through first-hand reports from those who had flown and fought with him during his heyday in Malta—my instructors at Aston Down in Gloucester, where I had taken my operational training during the previous winter. In fact Beurling had been regarded as a phenomenal pilot even before he made his name in Malta, when he trained at that same station—Aston Down—a year before me. On one occasion, "Screwball"—so nicknamed because he prefaced names, places, and items with that adjective—a mere student at the time, had astounded viewers when he flew a Spitfire on its back the full length of the runway, mere feet off the ground, finally rolling out of the inverted position, completing his circuit, and coming in for a perfect three-point landing. That unauthorized caper earned him a sharp reprimand—not the last he would receive by any means—from his superiors, who nevertheless remained in awe of this fledgling's talent.

All who knew Beurling talked not only of his skill but also of his unbelievable eyesight, his outstanding ability as a deflection shot (calculating the exact angle of fire)—the best in the world, some said—and his cool disregard for danger. In less than five months, he had become a legend, accounting for twenty-seven enemy planes destroyed, as well as one shared with two other pilots, nine probably destroyed, and three damaged. A true professional at his game, he was also thoroughly cold-blooded about it.

At a press conference held in the Parliament Buildings in Ottawa on November 9, 1942, when asked about his emotions at the height of battle, Beurling replied somberly,

I wonder if the enemy is going to blow or fry. There is no time for any other kind of thought. There is always someone on your tail and you have to be pretty sharp. There is no time to loiter around. You have to be hard-hearted, too. You must blaze away whenever you are in a position to get his oxygen bottles or gas tanks.

When Bruce West, a former columnist with the *Globe and Mail*, asked him if he'd ever shot down anyone in a parachute, he replied, "Damn right! Otherwise he might get down, get back to Germany, and come back and shoot *me* down."

Beurling had arrived at Biggin Hill under something of a cloud. After a hero's welcome in Canada, during which his transfer from the RAF to the RCAF had been arranged, he did a stint as a gunnery instructor before being posted to 403 Squadron RCAF of 127 Fighter Wing at Kenley fighter field, not far from Biggin Hill. He soon ran afoul of Hughie Godefroy, the wing commander, by stunting outside the CO's office at low level in the squadron's utility Tiger Moth—not just once, but three times in a row—even though he'd been warned to quit clowning around.

To make matters worse, when Godefroy took him to task, Beurling retorted belligerently, "You can't tell me what to do. That plane is under *my* command." Furious, Godefroy promptly placed him under open arrest, the first step toward a court martial, which he intended to enforce to the limit. It was an action that soared all the way to the top in the person of Charles "Chubby" Power, Canada's minister for Air.

Politically, this created a situation fraught with possible repercussions. On leave in Canada before returning overseas, Beurling received a hero's welcome in his hometown of Verdun, Quebec—earlier in Ottawa he had been crowned Canada's warrior prince by no less a dignitary than Prime Minister Mackenzie King himself. King was facing an overseas conscription crisis, and the last thing he needed was the spectacle of a court martial of Canada's fair-haired boy, whom he had personally endorsed.

The problem was solved by reducing the court martial charge to a temporary grounding and transferring him to our station—126 at Biggin Hill—under the flying leadership of the doughty, hard-driving Buck McNair, who had known Beurling from his own days in Malta. Both McNair and the discipline-minded airfield commander, Keith Hodson, could well cope with Beurling's reckless, non-conformist attitude and behaviour both in the air and on the ground. But there was a limit even to what these stalwarts would tolerate.

My own first impression of George (we never called him Buzz; that was a nickname dreamed up by the press) was of a somewhat reticent, soft-spoken loner, quite unlike our undisciplined image of him. He said to me, "I've always wanted to meet your father. I've studied his book [*Winged Warfare*] thoroughly. I'd like to have the opportunity of discussing air fighting with him and getting his ideas."

That meeting between the Lone Hawk of WWI and the Falcon of Malta (my father's designation of Beurling)—both rugged individualists when it came to air fighting—would have made interesting listening. Alas, it never took place.

As I got to know him better, I found George talkative and friendly, contrary to what some others thought. I liked him. He had a charisma that matched his fabulous record as an ace. His most striking feature was his eyes, a luminous blue, the whites somewhat speckled. When he wasn't grinning, his face, with its generous mouth and firm jaw, was a study in determination.

To me, George was a lot of fun and a great guy with the gals (we double-dated on several occasions). George, with his DSO, DFC, DFM, and medal ribbons under his RCAF wings, made me feel like a supernumerary, but it never really spoiled our evenings. In fact, George and I became good friends, and my admiration for him continued to grow.

My feelings, however, were not shared by all my sidekicks. Some of them considered him arrogant and aloof. One day in the officers' mess, George read aloud a particularly flowery—and rather sappy, too, in my opinion—letter from one of his girlfriends, a broad grin on his face, then crumpled it up and threw it into the fireplace. One of my brother officers angrily stomped out of the room, denouncing the performance as "thoughtless and vulgar."

Yet another of our confreres, Bob Hyndman, who had been my instructor when I was in training in Canada—and who later became noted as an official war artist—saw Beurling as something of a dreamer and found him as disarmingly gentle as I did. "There was something of the poet in him," Hyndman told me many years later. "The upturned collar of his battledress jacket, the longer-than-regulation haircut. But most of all, I was struck by his reluctance about being examined by an artist." This had a tinge of irony because Beurling's father was a commercial artist plying his trade in Montreal. George inherited some of that talent, though he never put it into practice—except to paint crosses on the engine cowling of his Spitfire denoting his many aerial victories.

Almost from the start of joining our outfit, George's exuberance and disregard for authority was bound to run into headwinds. Some of it was harmless enough and, at least in my opinion, worth a laugh. But not always.

George simply couldn't suppress his high spirits, no matter what he was up to. When he drove his pilots from the living quarters over to the dispersal in the heavy-duty truck, he would aim right at the hut at full speed—and at the last minute apply the brakes and deftly turn the wheels so that the vehicle came to a stop at an about-face, the back end facing the hut, depositing the pilots right at their front door, most of them somewhat shattered. To George it was all a big joke. It was also an example, albeit a hair-raising one, of his incredible sense of timing.

Another of his antics was even scarier. In the small officers' mess anteroom, he would stand with his back to the fireplace, throw a handful of shotgun shells into it, then make a dash for the door and, once outside, hold it shut while the rest of us dived for cover.

On the serious side, besides commanding his flight, George made himself useful teaching gunnery and visiting the other two squadrons in the wing, 411 and our own 401, casually discussing air-fighting tactics. My clearest recollection was of a discussion in which George preached the need to put everything into slow motion— a freeze-frame concept that allowed you to quickly size up the situation and take appropriate action, one that the great WWI American ace, Eddie Rickenbacker, called "the vision of the air."

While it was always fascinating to talk to Beurling about air fighting and his own experiences, it was obvious to us that this "slow motion" theory was more suitable to the Battle of Britain and Battle of Malta scenarios (not to mention the dogfights of 1914–18), which inevitably produced lone-wolf one-on-one duels, than to our present style of operations over the occupied countries of Western Europe. Our mandate was bomber-escort sorties, a defensive measure, as well as search-and-destroy forays limited to finding the odd unsuspecting German *Jagdstaffel* (squadron). But most often our quarry was German bombers flown to advanced airfields to arm and refuel for night raids over England (the "Little Blitz" of the winter of 1943–44), which we'd catch both on the ground and in the air.

On one occasion, and one only, even though we were with different squadrons, I had the enviable experience of making a practice flight with George, who taught me a lesson that many months later probably saved my life. Over breakfast one morning, he asked, "Care to take a flip with me?"—an offer I couldn't refuse. With my commanding officer's permission, I rendezvoused with George at the end of the runway to take off for a tail-chase, a follow-the-leader exercise.

I was pretty excited because I prided myself that through much practice, I was able to stick to the leader through thick or thin no matter what manoeuvre he put me through. But I wasn't prepared for what George had in store.

For starters, I followed George through the usual procedures of slow rolls, loops, rolls off the top of the loop, twisting dives, spiral climbs, steep turns, and so on—no trouble at all. Then—suddenly, and when I least expected it—George pulled up sharply, cut his throttle, flicked around, zoomed past above me, rolled out, and ended up on my tail, all in a matter of seconds.

Over the radio transmitter, he laughed, "Got you, eh? That's a stunt that can get you out of a whole lot of trouble if a Hun gets up your ass," he said. "Follow me and I'll show you how to do it."

For the next twenty minutes, I clung to his tail like glue while George patiently put me through the paces. Varying the throttle thrust, spiralling, whipping from one side to the other, then climbing and twisting, George gradually increased the tempo each time. It was a tough routine. I was sweating, trying to stay in place, but finally I had the pattern pretty well down pat, and I later practised it diligently. But George cautioned me: "It won't do a bit of good unless you keep a sharp lookout.

Keep turning your head—up, down, and sideways—so you won't get bounced by surprise." (An echo of what my father once told me: "I rubbed the back of my neck raw from my collar just twisting and turning so no one could get the jump on me.")

Inevitably, George's independent attitude and casual disregard and disrespect for rules and regulations would clash with authority. Two blatant examples come readily to mind.

From dawn until breakfast time, a flight from each of the squadrons took turns standing readiness against an enemy raid, prepared to "scramble" into the air at a moment's notice when the alarm sounded. Beurling flatly announced to his flight that this was a lot of nonsense. "To hell with it! The Battle of Britain ended four years ago," he said and told them to ignore the order, to the fury of his CO, George Keefer. Buck McNair, the wingco, had him on the carpet and told him the order must be obeyed.

On another occasion, while on one of our search-and-destroy sweeps, George took his flight (consisting of four Spitfires, including his own) on a private crusade, breaking off from the rest of the wing, though he'd been warned countless times that our emphasis was on team work and to cut out that "stupid lone eagle stuff." That was bad enough. What made matters worse was that he kept his flight stooging about, looking for prey to the limit of their fuel endurance. On reaching the English coast, one of the pilots had to force land onto a pasture when his fuel ran out. Another stiff reprimand for Beurling issued from Keefer and McNair, with Keith Hodson looking on disapprovingly.

But there was much worse to come.

From the beginning of 1944, the air war over Europe changed dramatically. With the introduction of the long-range American P-51 (Mustang) fighter to escort the Flying Fortress daylight raids against Germany, the aerial battles now took place over the Fatherland. That's where the action was, and that was where George Frederick Beurling was determined to be. He might have pulled it off, too, but for his penchant for thumbing his nose at official orders.

Somehow, despite his capriciousness, he managed to wangle permission to lead a flight of Spitfires equipped with 80-gallon long-range drop tanks on a fighter sweep into the Ruhr. The plan was to fly in at deck level, under radar range. Therein lay the root of the problem. Frequently, when switching over on takeoff to the disposable tanks from the main fuel tanks, an air lock would develop that could result in a crash. Orders were therefore issued to climb to 1,000 feet before switching over. On this occasion, Beurling instructed his pilots to ignore the regulation and once in the air to stay at ground level to avoid enemy radar detection. A bit ridiculous to assume the takeoff of a mere four aircraft hundreds of miles to the west would raise any sort of alarm on the part of the German radar operators.

In this case, it had fatal consequences. Switching over, the engine of the tail man in Beurling's flight packed up, and he crashed into the shallow valley at the end of the runway and was killed. Aborting the flight, Beurling landed and drove over to the site of the accident, only to find that McNair and Hodson had already reached the scene. Apparently, there was a heated exchange of words over the affair, which I later pieced together, and Beurling was subsequently grounded, posted off the wing, and sent home.

Whatever was said can only be conjectured, but many months later one of the pilots from my squadron, whom I ran into at the repatriation depot near Liverpool, told me that Beurling said to him, "All I need is twenty rounds and McNair can have all the ammunition he wants." Bitter words. Shortly after his return to Canada, Beurling was discharged from the RCAF.

I never saw George again after he left Biggin Hill, but I heard that he had not adjusted to civilian life. His heart was still in the skies, the milieu he loved and in which he had acquitted himself so gallantly in combat. It seems fitting that he would try once again to find his way into battle. In 1947, he turned his restlessness into action by volunteering to fight with the Israeli Air Force.

Before I left for my office in Montreal on the morning of Thursday, May 20, 1948, Billy Edwards (son of Air Marshal Harold Edwards, former RCAF overseas chief of staff), then a reporter with the *Montreal Star,* phoned to tell me, "Your friend George Beurling's been killed flying a Norseman from Urbe airfield, north of Rome." He went on; "I've got a great quote from his father saying that he always expected his son's life 'would end in a blaze of smoke from the thing he loved most, the airplane.'"

So ended the life of the man that Laddie Lucas, who fought alongside George in Malta, described as "probably the most brilliant individual fighter pilot of the two world wars . . . [a] man I came to know and so much admired."

I feel the same way.

Arthur Bishop
Toronto
September 2001

FLYING OFFICER GEORGE F. BEURLING